PENGUIN COOKERY LIF

G000048216

A Harvest c,
Apples

Ruth Ward was born in Edinburgh and graduated in Modern Languages from St Andrews University before taking a Dip. Ed. in Dundee. She first developed her interest in European cuisine while spending time as a student at Bonn University, and since then has travelled widely in Europe. A part-time teacher, she lives in Oxfordshire with her doctor husband and two sons. *A Harvest of Apples* is her first book and combines her interests in cookery, literature and history.

RUTH WARD

A HARVEST OF APPLES

PENGUIN BOOKS

PENGUIN BOOKS

Published by the Penguin Group
27 Wrights Lane, London w8 5tz, England
Viking Penguin Inc., 40 West 23rd Street, New York, New York 10010, USA
Penguin Books Australia Ltd, Ringwood, Victoria, Australia
Penguin Books Canada Ltd, 2801 John Street, Markham, Ontario, Canada l3r 1b4
Penguin Books (NZ) Ltd, 182–190 Wairau Road, Auckland 10, New Zealand

Penguin Books Ltd, Registered Offices: Harmondsworth, Middlesex, England

First published 1988

Filmset in 10/12½ Linotron Goudy by
Rowland Phototypesetting Ltd, Bury St Edmunds, Suffolk
Printed and bound in Great Britain by
Richard Clay Ltd, Bungay, Suffolk
Designed by Judith Gordon

Contents

Acknowledgements

My thanks are due, first and foremost, to my husband, John, and my sons, Charles and Adrian, for the help and encouragement they have given me, and for trying out the recipes.

I am also most grateful to the following who have given me recipes: Elsa Klein, Lisbeth Weber, Maria Pjede, Ursula Sieweke, Véronique Vorng-Vancorselis, Birgit Sørensen, Mrs D. Macleod and Mrs K. Morgan; also the staff of the Bodleian Library and the Radcliffe Science Library, Oxford, the Ministry of Agriculture, Fisheries and Food, the National Seed Development Organization Ltd, the Agricultural and Food Research Council Institute of Horticultural Research, East Malling, H. P. Bulmer Ltd, The Museum of Cider, Hereford, and the Farm Shop and Pick Your Own Association Ltd.

Golden Pippins. t. 4.

Sold by Mr. Wagner at Seigr. Amiconis in Great Marlborough Street. According to Act of Parliament C.P.E.S.

Introduction

There grew a goodly tree him faire beside,
Loaden with fruit and apples rosy redd,
As they in pure vermilion had been dide,
Whereof great vertues over-all were redd;
For happy life to all which thereon fedd,
And life eke everlasting did befall:
Great God it planted in that blessed stedd
With His Almighty hand, and did it call
The tree of life, the crime of our first fathers fall.

EDMUND SPENSER,
The Faerie Queene

here can be few more depressing sights than an apple tree in late autumn, its branches laden with over-ripe fruit, some already rotting, while around its roots lie windfalls which are providing food only for maggots and wasps. Yet this is an all-too-frequent sight, both in gardens and hedgerows. Equally frustrating is the news of large quantities of apples having to be pulped as it is uneconomic to sell them cheaply.

It seems strange that so many people fail to take advantage of this delicious fruit which grows freely in their gardens and in its wild form. Perhaps they cannot be bothered to pick them, or they do not know how to store them, or it may simply be that they think there is no more to apple cookery than pies and crumbles. But this is not so. Although the apple is our most common fruit, it has a fascinating history and limitless versatility in a wide variety of dishes.

This book contains a selection of my favourite apple recipes, both traditional and new, from home and abroad, all tried and tested. I hope it will save time-consuming searching through general cookery books and supply new ideas to those who need inspiration in using up large quantities of apples!

1

About Apples

Their fruit were golden apples glistring bright,
    That goodly was their glory to behold;
    On earth like never grew, ne living wight
Like ever saw, but they from hence were sold;
For those which Hercules, with conquest bold
Got from great Atlas daughters, hence began,
    And planted there did bring forth fruit of gold;
And those with which th' Euboean young man wan
Swift Atalanta, when through craft he her out ran.

Here also sprong that goodly golden fruit,
    With which Acontius got his lover trew,
Whom he had long time sought with fruitlesse suit:
    Here eke that famous golden Apple grew
The which emongst the gods false Ate threw;
    For which th'Idaean Ladies disagreed,
    Till partiall Paris dempt it Venus dew,
And had of her fayre Helen for his meed,
That many noble Greekes and Trojans made to bleed.

EDMUND SPENSER,
The Faerie Queene

pples tend to be associated with temptation and seduc-tion. Eve, Atalanta and Snow White neglected duty, principle and safety respectively when lured by an apple, while the goddesses Hera, Aphrodite and Athene strove to impress Paris for the prize of the Apple of Discord. Did the appeal result from the bright colouring of the skin, or the crisp, juicy flesh, or was it simply because the apple is so delightfully uncomplicated? Unlike fruits which must be peeled or stoned, or which leave the fingers sticky, the ripe apple can be picked and enjoyed straight from the tree.

Perhaps it is this factor above all which has made the purloining of apples such a temptation throughout the ages. Traditionally, this is a masculine role! Adam took the apple from the tree of knowledge, Hercules stole the golden apples of the Hesperides as one of his twelve labours, while the Norse giant Thiazi demanded the goddess Idunn and her magic apples of youth as a ransom for Loki. Since then there have been countless smaller and less distinguished scrumpers.

Yet despite its charms, the apple is not a particularly nutritious fruit. It contains comparatively little vitamin C, and any prolonged soaking, cooking or warming, especially of apple purée, can com-pletely destroy the vitamin content. Ironically, the most vitamin-rich variety is a cooker, the Bramley's Seedling. The apple's nutritional merits are two-fold. Firstly, it contains fibre, which is essential to good digestion, and secondly, it is low in calories, therefore useful in weight-reducing diets. Mrs Beeton sums it up in this typically practical statement:

All apples contain sugar, malic acid, or the acid of apples; mucilage, or gum; woody fibre, and water; together with some aroma, on which their peculiar flavour depends. The hard acid kinds are unwholesome if eaten raw; but by the process of cooking, a great deal of this acid is decomposed and converted into sugar. The sweet and mellow kinds form a valuable addition to the dessert.

Brillat-Savarin also commends it for its sleep-inducing qualities thus:

Some kinds of food gently provoke sleep . . . especially the rennet apple when eaten immediately before retiring to rest.

There are now over three thousand different types of apple, dessert apples and cookers, some readily available from nurseries and garden centres, others almost forgotten, surviving only in old gardens. No attempt to classify them has been wholly successful as there are too many intermediates and overlaps; however, in his book *A Handbook of Hardy Fruits* (1920), Edward Bunyard classed them into seven separate colour groups, giving an example of each as the title: Lord Derby, Lane's Prince Albert, Peasgood's Nonsuch, Golden Noble, Baumanns, Cox's Orange Pippin and Russet. Another expert, Harold Taylor, writing about the same time, also classified them by colour but included flavour.

Bunyard lists a host of pippins, reinettes, russets, pearmains and codlins, but very few of them would feature in the modern nursery catalogue. The reason is that, sadly, many of the most delicious and subtly flavoured apples are unsuited to commercial mass production and as a result have simply died out. Our growers now have to compete with a flood of imports, mainly French Golden Delicious – the ideal commercial variety: it can be stored for months in gas-filled chambers without any sign of deterioration. This enables the crop to be released gradually and prices to be maintained. Some Cox's Orange Pippins are now being picked before they are ripe and treated in this way; as a result they are small and tasteless, bearing little resemblance to the delectable true version. Whereas the aromatic Beauty of Bath was once our most widely grown dessert apple, the choice today, especially in urban areas, is often limited to Golden Delicious and Cox's which have been treated in this unappealing way. Only certain farm shops and orchards still offer a wide choice.

Although the Golden Delicious is considered a French apple nowadays, it originated as a chance seedling in West Virginia. From this humble origin it achieved fame in 1959 when a Missouri nursery bought a tree for $51,000 (then c. £18,200), the highest price ever paid for any tree. Today, many English growers have discarded their traditional varieties, replacing them with the more profitable Golden Delicious trees. Fortunately, English gardens remain a haven for older varieties – a neglected feature of our heritage.

How did so many different varieties come into existence? There are basically two ways of propagating apples: raising them from seed, in which case a new variety will be produced each time, and vegetative

1 Striped Juneating
2 Summer Oslin
3 Kerry Pippin
4 Summer Pippin
5 Tartarian Crab
6 Duchess of Oldenburgh

propagation, i.e. propagation by budding or grafting on to rootstock, reproducing the variety from which the cutting has been taken. In addition, a 'sport' or spontaneous mutation may form on a parent stock and produce a new variety, for example Queen Cox from Cox's Orange Pippin, Red Ellison from Ellison's Orange.

Apples raised from seed fall into two categories: those whose parentage is unknown, which are usually the products of amateur planting or a chance seeding, like the Golden Delicious, and those produced by crossing, the results of careful breeding by professional growers. Apples do not breed true from seed, so any pip which germinates will produce a new variety, but these are of variable quality. Nevertheless it is by this method that a large number of our finest apples have come into being. Since ancient times they have been growing wild all over Europe and were popular in Britain long before the Roman invasion, shedding their pips and begetting new varieties. Indeed, the orchards of the West Country are said to have sprung from pips discarded by Joseph of Arimathea at Glastonbury Tor, and the orchards of Normandy, according to legend, owe their origin to the pips of the Apple of Discord. The nymph Thetis, remembering how the dispute over this apple had disrupted her wedding celebrations, felt jealous and angry at her exclusion from the ensuing beauty contest at which Paris awarded the apple to Aphrodite. Following the goddess to the Norman coast, she stole the fruit, devoured it and scattered the pips along the coast. A more down-to-earth explanation in both cases is that pomace, the pounded pulp and cores from which juice had been extracted, was spread in the pastures as manure, and must have resulted in large numbers of seedlings. Also, large quantities of apple trees were brought to Britain by the Normans after 1066.

Many pips planted by amateurs have also resulted in famous varieties. The Ribston Pippin, discovered at Ribston Hall, Knaresborough, in 1709, is said to have been grown from a pip brought from Rouen. The Blenheim Orange, which first came to notice in 1818, was grown from a pip by Mr Kempster, a cottager at Woodstock whose garden adjoined Blenheim Park. One of our most popular dessert apples, the Cox's Orange Pippin, was raised in this way by Richard Cox, a retired brewer, in his garden at Colnbrook in 1825, while Matthew Bramley, a Nottinghamshire shoemaker, gave

The Orange Pippin.

his name to the Bramley's Seedling, our most popular cooking apple, although the pip was actually planted by a Miss Mary Brailsford, a previous owner of Mr Bramley's cottage in Southwell.

Crossing was first carried out by Thomas Knight (1758–1838), who conducted a series of experiments, using the pollen of one variety to fertilize another. From the pips of the resulting fruit he raised seedlings whose parentage was known, and it was thus possible to determine which varieties inter-crossed best, which were self-fertile or self-sterile, which were most resistant to disease, and which were good pollen or seed parents. The Cox's Orange Pippin has been used frequently in both roles, and from it have resulted many fine varieties – Laxton's Superb, Laxton's Epicure, Tydeman's Late Orange and Sunset, to name but a few.

Vegetative propagation, the second method mentioned above, involves budding or grafting cuttings on to a different rootstock. In this case, the new young tree will produce the same fruit as the tree from which the cutting was taken. Vegetative propagation involves cloning as opposed to natural reproduction. Thus cuttings from the original Ribston Pippin tree were taken to Brompton Park Nursery, and in 1785, seventy-six years after the discovery of the original tree, twenty-five trees were listed there. Mr Cox's tree was first recognized by Charles Turner of the Royal Nurseries, Slough (after whose son the Arthur Turner cooking apple is named), and he took cuttings from it. The famous tree was unfortunately blown down in 1911, but by then it had outgrown its useful life and its cuttings had already become large mature Cox's trees. The Cox's Orange Pippin has since become what many connoisseurs consider the finest dessert apple in the world. One such was Edward Bunyard, who coined the term 'coxomaniac'.

It is thanks to vegetative propagation that good varieties, once raised, can be perpetuated. The Annurca, a red apple grown in the Naples district, was mentioned by Pliny in AD 101 and is still a vigorous cropper. Two other varieties mentioned in books in the seventeenth century – the Court Pendu Plat in 1611 and the Devonshire Quarrenden in 1685 – are still grown today, and the former, crossed with the Cox's Orange Pippin, has produced the Laxton's Royalty.

A large number of superior varieties were introduced to Britain by the Romans. They esteemed the fruit greatly, and Mrs Beeton notes that certain well-known Roman families gave their names to their favourite apples, e.g. Manlians, Claudians and Appians. A better-known Roman import was the *pomme d'api* or lady-apple, described by Martin Lister in *A Journey to Paris in the Year 1690* as 'a small flat apple, very beautiful, red on one side and pale or white on the other, and may serve the Ladies at their Toilets a Pattern to Paint by'. The best varieties were later cultivated in monastery gardens, and by the end of the thirteenth century the Royal Gardens at Westminster, Charing and the Tower, as well as the gardens of several wealthy noblemen, could boast a large selection of choice apples. Two of these were the pearmain and the costard.

The pearmain, which takes its name from its long pear-like form, is the first named variety recorded in English history, and was probably our main dessert apple for centuries. It is mentioned in a deed of 1204 relating to the holding of the lordship of Runham in Norfolk, for which an annual payment of two hundred pearmains was due to the Exchequer on the feast of St Michael. Anthony Wood, the antiquarian, records in 1663: 'for a peck of peermanes, 6d; given to Mary to fetch them 1d'. Today the Worcester pearmain is the best known of this family.

The costard is the oldest variety of cooking apple. Grown extensively in the reign of Edward I, it was popular for pies until well after Shakespeare's time. The name probably derives from old French *coste*, a rib, as this was a prominent feature of the costard. A Kentish grower, advertising his wares in 1892, described the Martin's Costard as 'a very large apple, shape oval, very much ribbed'. It was probably similar in appearance to the Calville, a Norman apple, characterized by ribbed sides at the neck. In 1296 costards were sold in Oxford market for a shilling per hundred; in 1325 twenty-nine costard trees fetched three shillings. Compare this with the record price paid for the Golden Delicious tree! Unfortunately costards have virtually disappeared today: as early as 1853 Robert Hogg wrote, 'the true costard is now rarely to be met with', and Bunyard's list includes only one, the Pope's Scarlet. Shakespeare called the clown in *Love's Labour Lost* Costard, and the name also survives in the word coster-monger, originally a purveyor of apples.

Another cooking variety is the codlin, mentioned by Shakespeare in *Twelfth Night*. The name derives from the culinary term 'coddle' or parboil, as this was the most popular method of cooking codlins. Originally the name was applied to any small immature green apple, which was parboiled whole and then skinned, but by Elizabethan times the old English Codlin was being cultivated as a distinct variety. A favourite dish of the period was 'codlins and cream' and this name is still used by country folk for the great willowherb. Another well-known recipe was hot codlins, roasted apples sold hot in the streets of London. A popular song of Grimaldi, written in 1825, contains these lines:

> A little old woman her living she got
> By selling hot codlins, hot, hot, hot.

Pippins are dessert apples, and their name is generally taken to mean 'raised from pips', although in his *Treatise of Cyder* (1691) Worlidge states that 'pippins take their name from the small spots or pips that usually appear on the sides of the apple'. Their French name is reinette, as in 'Apples called reinettes or pippins, the bushel xijd' (Rates of Customs, 1853). Although there are references to the pippin before 1500, it was in this year that Robert Harris, Henry VIII's fruiterer, 'fetched out of France a great store of grafts, especially pippins, before which there were no pippins in England'. Vendors of these apples were known as pippinmongers, but the term has not survived as 'costermonger' has. Yet Andrew Tuer's book, *Old London Street Cries* (1885), records many examples of their cries, e.g. 'Roasted pippins piping hot', 'Piepin pys' or simply 'Pippins!' and includes a sad ballad about a girl pippinmonger who fell into the Thames, but who still cries out her wares!

Another apple of French origin is the Nonpareil, recognized only at the beginning of the eighteenth century, but said to have originated from seeds brought from France and planted by the Jesuits in Elizabethan times. Its English name is Nonsuch.

In 1525 Leonard Mascal established an orchard at Plumstead and as well as supplying the London markets with apples, he also sold grafts to wealthy landowners who wanted to increase their collections of fruit trees. It is largely to them that we owe our heritage of so many choice varieties. One such was Shallow, who, in *Henry IV, Part II*, shows off his garden to his friends thus: 'Now you shall see my orchard where, in an arbour, we will eat a last year's pippin of my own

THE COSTER-GIRL.

"Apples! An 'aypenny a lot, Apples!"

[*From a Daguerreotype by* BEARD.]

grafting.' This was probably an anachronism, since Henry IV's reign came to an end in 1413, almost a century before Harris imported the grafts, but it serves to illustrate Shakespeare's interest in current innovations.

The last words of this section must go to Edward Bunyard, who sums up his thoughts on apples thus:

It is significant that the apple has given its best to the Nordic nations and it is among them that it is specially esteemed. Exceptions there are, of course, but against Jargellon, King of Poland, who fled at the sight of this fruit, we may set the fact that Schiller found his best inspiration in the scent of apples.

The
Traditional Apple Calendar

As well as receiving frequent mentions in our literature, the apple's contribution to our heritage can be seen in the number of place-names which bear the prefix 'apple' – Appleby, Appledore, Appleton, etc., and, going back into legend, the fabled Avalon or 'isle of apples' whither King Arthur was borne after his last battle.

The fruit is an intrinsic feature of many ancient picturesque customs and traditions, as the following calendar shows.

NEW YEAR WASSAILING

Young women went from house to house with seasonally decorated wassail bowls singing carols:

> Our Wassail we do fill
> With apples and with spice,
> Then grant us your goodwill
> To taste here once or twice
> Of our good Wassail.

'Wassail' comes from the Saxon term *waes hael*, meaning 'be in good health', and is the origin of the toast. But in this ceremony the term was sometimes confused with 'vessel'.

17 JANUARY (OLD TWELFTH NIGHT): WASSAILING THE ORCHARDS

It was said that this West Country custom would promote a good harvest, while failure to carry it out could lead to ill luck or loss of the entire crop. The farmer, his family, friends and neighbours met in the

Wassailing

orchard with a pitcher of cider full of roasted apples. Dancing around the largest or the most productive tree, they recited this toast three times:

> Here's to thee, old apple tree
> Whence thou mayst bud and thou mayst blow!
> And whence thou mayst bear apples enow!
> Hats full! Caps full!
> Bushel, bushel sacks full!
> And my pockets full too, huzza!

Then they sprinkled the trees with cider. There are many variations of this custom. In some areas, toast or cakes soaked in cider were hung on the trees or placed on a large bough for the robins, their guardian spirits. Occasionally a little boy was lifted into the tree to represent this guardian and was handed bread, cheese and cider. Sometimes the branches of the tree were dipped in the cider. In each case, the ceremony represents a sort of primitive sacrament in which the tree, or its spirit, is blessed and given food and drink to sustain it and ensure its fruitfulness.

In recent years this ancient ritual has been revived by the Taunton Cider Company and is performed at Monty's Court, Norton Fitz-warren, near Taunton, the home of Major Mitford-Slade. A Wassail Queen now performs the rituals with the toast and cider, and a brass band accompanies the wassailing song.

COLLOP MONDAY, SHROVE TUESDAY, FRITTER WEDNESDAY

On the eve of Shrove Tuesday, boys used to go through the streets knocking on doors with clubs. On Shrove Tuesday they repeated this procedure, accompanying it with rhymes begging for apples and pancakes or dumplings:

> Shrovetide is nigh at hand
> And we are come a-shroving.
> Pray, dame, give something,
> An apple or a dumpling.

In some parts of the country this also took place on Fritter Wednesday (Ash Wednesday). There is a reference to the custom in the second verse of 'Oranges and Lemons'.

> 'Pancakes and fritters,' say the bells of St Peter's,
> 'Two sticks and an apple,' say the bells of Whitechapel.

The second line refers to the clubs beating the doors and the subsequent request.

23 JUNE – MIDSUMMER DAY

A picturesque annual custom of auctioning common land by the medium of apples used to be observed on the Saturday before old Midsummer Day in the village of Ruxton, Somerset. Two large areas, named the East and West Dolemoors, were divided into portions called furlongs. On each of twenty-four apples a distinctive tra-ditional mark was cut, e.g. a pole-axe, cross, fork, oxen and mare or duck's nest. The apples were then put into a bag and the furlongs divided into acres. Then a boy took out the apples one by one and their marks were cut into the acres. Each villager, recognizing his mark, claimed his allotment for the year. The custom was discontinued in 1811 when the land was enclosed and allotted in perpetuity.

BLESSING THE APPLES

John Aubrey records in *Remaines of Gentilisme* (1696) that 'in Herefordshire and also in Somersetshire, on Midsommer-eve, they make fires in the Fields and in the waies: *sc.* to Blesse the Apples'.

This was also done in some localities on St James' Day, 25 July. Midsummer Day is the festival of St James' brother, St John.

15 JULY – ST SWITHIN'S DAY

In Hampshire people believed that it was wrong to eat an apple before this date. Nor should the early windfalls of the 'June drop' be made into jelly because, until christened by St Swithin, they were regarded not as proper apples but as fairies' food. Rain on St Swithin's Day meant that the saint was christening the apples and a good harvest was ensured.

25 AUGUST – APPLE-PIE FAIR

Apple-pie Fairs are held in Marldon, Devon, in memory of a local farmer, George Hill, who every year gave windfalls to his workers and an enormous apple pie to the village fair. Nowadays an apple-pie princess is chosen and crowned.

THIRD SATURDAY OF SEPTEMBER – CUMBERLAND CRAB FAIR

Since the year 1267, the Cumberland Crab Fair has been held on this day, at the season when crab apples are ripe. It was the occasion when the lord of the manor received tithes and distributed gifts to the crowd.

29 SEPTEMBER – MICHAELMAS

To Michaelmas belong two apple customs, each quite different in character, belonging to different parts of the country, but both wasteful.

Devonshire village girls used to gather crab apples from the hedgerows, take them to a loft and arrange them in the form of their lovers' initials. Those found to be in the best condition on Michaelmas Day indicated the couple most likely to wed.

Michaelmas Day was the day of the election of the bailiff in Kidderminster; 'Kellums', the lawless hour, occurred between the retiral of one bailiff and the accession of his successor. The latter, accompanied by the corporation, walked to the house of the retiring bailiff, followed by an unruly mob of citizens throwing apples at the procession.* This custom was abolished at the end of the eighteenth century.

Hallowe'en – ducking for apples

This may be related to the custom called Crab Wake or Kenelm's Wake, held in the village of St Kenelm's, also in Worcestershire. Here people pelt each other with crab apples.

31 OCTOBER –
HALLOWE'EN OR SNAPAPPLE NIGHT

On 1 November the Romans held a feast to Pomona, goddess of fruits and seeds. Hence the association of apples and nuts with Hallowe'en. Lambswool, originally La Mas Ubhal, meaning the day of the apple fruit, was drunk, and games involving apples were played. One was the ever-popular ducking or bobbing for apples, in which the fruits are retrieved by mouth from a tub of water. Another involved the use of a

stick, suspended horizontally by a string, with an apple at one end and a lighted candle at the other. The stick was whirled round and the player had to try to catch the apple with his teeth.

Apples were also used in divination games, usually for guessing one's future marriage partner, as already seen in the Michaelmas custom. Here are three Hallowe'en divination games:

1. If a girl ate an apple alone in front of a mirror she might look over her shoulder for the reflection of her future husband's face.
2. Two cut apple pips were stuck on the eyelids or cheeks to help to choose between two suitors. The pips were named after them and the one which fell off first was proved inconstant.
3. The girl peeled an apple, swung the peel three times round her head and dropped it. It was supposed to fall in the shape of her lover's initial. Sometimes this rhyme accompanied the action:

> I pare this pippin round and round again
> My sweetheart's name to flourish on the plain.
> I fling the unbroken paring o'er my head,
> My sweetheart's letter on the ground is read.

23 NOVEMBER – ST CLEMENT'S DAY, OR BITE-APPLE DAY

Clemening, or house-to-house begging for apples, was practised first by blacksmiths and later by children in rural England. As Clement was said to be the son of St Catherine, whose feast falls on 25 November, her name was sometimes included in the clemening rhymes:

> Clemany! Clemany! Clemany! Mine!
> A good red apple and a pint of wine!
> (Staffordshire)

> Cattern and Clemen be here,
> here, here,
> Give us your apples and give us your
> beer!
> (Sussex)

25 DECEMBER – CHRISTMAS DAY

Before the days of coloured baubles, red apples used to adorn Christmas trees, especially in Germany, where the Christmas tree custom originated. In 1605 an anonymous writer described a

Christmas tree in Strasbourg, then a German city, as decorated with paper flowers, apples, gold foil, wafers and sweets. In Britain, prior to the introduction of the tree by Prince Albert in 1840, a traditional Christmas decoration was the Kissing Bough, a garland of greenery and mistletoe hung with red apples and candles.

A custom known as worsting, howling or youling, similar to wassailing, was practised in the western and southern counties and some parts of Wales on Christmas morning. Those taking part were called howlers and they were led by a trumpeter with a ram's horn. Instead of sprinkling the trees, the howlers rapped them with clubs to the accompaniment of the ram's horn, thus frightening away malevolent spirits. After these proceedings they sang for admission to the farmer's house, where they were fêted with ale. *

Variations on these themes occur in other countries. In some districts of France, for example, the Lenten ceremony of Grannas-mias served a similar purpose: flaming torches were applied to the apple trees or passed under their branches by children under the age of twelve, to ensure a good crop. In south Germany the tablecloths were carried out to the orchards after the Christmas meal and the crumbs shaken over the apple-tree roots, again to ensure the next year's harvest.

The strangest superstition of all, once firmly believed in central European countries, was that an apple tree should be planted at the birth of a male child. The subsequent health of both child and tree were thereafter said to be interlinked – an example of sympathetic magic which must have caused much needless anxiety. Far better our wassailing and Hallowe'en games where the superstitions are light-hearted and give pleasure to the participants.

> There is one creed: 'neath no world-terror's wing
> Apples forget to grow on apple trees.
> G. K. Chesterton, 'Ecclesiastes'

* Much of this variation probably occurred through the change of the calendar in 1582, when the Christmas festival was moved from Epiphany (Twelfth Night) to 25 December and Twelfth Night to 6 January. In some areas the wassailing ceremony moved with Christmas; in others the old date was retained. The discrepancy of eleven to thirteen days between the old and new festivals was caused by the fact that 1700 and 1800 were leap years in the Julian Calendar, but common ones in the Gregorian.

2
Which Variety?

I said to heart, 'How goes it?' He replied,
'Right as a Ribston pippin.'

HILAIRE BELLOC

The Alexander Apple.

ike the street-vendors of old London, early cookery writers usually specified which variety of apple should be used. For instance, Robert May, author of *The Accomplish'd Cook* (1660), gives recipes for 'Pippin Pye' and 'Codlins and Cream', among others, the reader being directed to take 'twenty fair codlins' or 'thirty good large pippins'. *The British Cookery Book* (1883) by John Walsh directs the cook to 'take some prettily formed apples of the pearmain or nonsuch kind' and even 'middling-sized Kentish pippins'. The cook was left in no doubt as to the variety needed!

Apart from crab and cider apples, which form classes of their own, apples fall into two categories: cookers and desserts. Cookers provide the main ingredient for basic apple purée and are also used in the majority of hot dishes. The most popular cooker, and the variety most readily available in the shops, is the Bramley's Seedling. There are, however, many other excellent varieties including Grenadier, Revd W. Wilkes, Lord Derby, Golden Noble, Emneth Early, Monarch and Lane's Prince Albert. Young trees of these varieties can be bought from most nursery gardens.

When a recipe calls for a dessert apple to be cooked, pippins (or reinettes) are most suitable. They have a firm enough texture to be poached whole or cooked in slices without breaking. A soft juicy apple would simply disintegrate in these conditions. Pippins are therefore the ideal variety for recipes in which dessert apples are poached or stuffed and baked. Cox's are always easily obtainable, Sturmers are sometimes on sale early in the year, or you may be fortunate enough to have a Ribston or Allington pippin tree in your garden. Golden Delicious and Granny Smiths can also be used. Pippins are also suitable for pies and tarts, as are James Grieves and Blenheim Oranges.

In some recipes however, especially salads, a green- or red-skinned apple may be required. Here the appearance is an important factor; if you are buying apples for such a recipe, the most suitable green apples are Greensleeves, Granny Smith and Crispin, while Discovery, Idared, Worcester Pearmain, Tydeman's Early Worcester,

Spartan and Red Ellison are a few of the choice red-skinned varieties.

Some apples can be used as desserts or cookers, e.g. Newton Wonder, Peasgood's Nonsuch and James Grieve, of which Bunyard wrote that it 'makes a pie full of subtle memories'.

Meg Dods' *Cook and Housewife's Manual* (1826) offers sound advice on cooking with apples.

A variety of apples besides codlins are used for baking, though russetings, Ribstone pippins, golden pippins and such as melt equally and are a little acid, are esteemed the best. Apple pie used to be seasoned with pounded cinnamon and cloves; now lemon-grate, quince marmalade, candied citron or orange peel, are preferred. If the apples have become dry and insipid, the parings and cores may be boiled with a stick of cinnamon and sugar, and the strained liquor added to the pie.

To this list of seasonings and complementary flavourings may be added sage, rosemary, orange-flower water, rosewater, nutmeg, ginger, mixed spice, dried fruit and almost any fresh fruit.

For further information on varieties see the appendix 'Apple Index' on p. 227.

What wond'rous life is this I lead!
Ripe apples drop about my head.
Andrew Marvell, 'The Garden'

3

Storage of Apples

Are they spectres, those apples
ranged like flags and banners all in battle order,
row after row, in the storeroom?

CHARLES DE COSTER,
Tyl Ulenspiegel

1. The Breedon Pippin.   2. The Lamb Abbey Pearmain.
3. The Braddick Nonpareil.   4. The Pomeroy Pippin Nonpareil.

1820

o one gave more thorough advice on the gathering and storage of apples than the multi-talented Elizabethan poet, Gervase Markham, in *The English Huswife* (1683). He wrote that apples 'must be gathered on a fair, sunny and dry day in the wane of the Moon, and no wind in the East, also after the dew is gone away for the least wet or moisture will make them subject to rot and mildew'. And on storage:

> Apples that are not of like colour should not be laid together, and if any such be mingled, let it be amended, and those which are ripe first, let them be first spent, and to that end, lay those apples together that are of one time of ripening, and thus you must use Pippins also, yet will they endure bruises better than another fruit, and whilst they are green will heal another.
>
> If you spy any rotten fruit in your heaps, pick them out . . . leave not a tainted Apple in them, dividing the hardest by themselves, and the broken skinned by themselves to be first spent.

The elegant language of Markham expresses a great deal of practical wisdom which is still valid today.

Apples should not be picked until their stalks part readily from the branch. To test this, lift the apple on the palm of your hand and gently twist the stalk – if the apple is ripe it will detach itself easily from the branch. Apples should never be pulled with force or broken from their branches, nor should the stalk be removed.

Early and second early varieties* do not generally keep well and should be used as soon as possible. Some, such as Discovery and James Grieve, will start to shrivel quite soon; others, including Laxton's Fortune and Worcester Pearmain, will keep rather longer.

Mid-season apples, which ripen in October, and late apples may be stored into the following year, but care must be taken to ensure that the fruit is sound and free from bruises, blemishes or any damage inflicted by wasps or grubs. The skin should be dry and the stalk intact. Damaged apples should be used up at once; if stored they only affect adjacent ones. Large or very small fruits should also be used up quickly as they do not keep as well as medium-sized ones.

* See p. 227 for details of ripening seasons.

Apples should be stored in a cool, dark, airy place such as a garage, shed or well-ventilated cellar. Wrap each fruit separately in a piece of newspaper or tissue-paper and spread them out on trays or in slatted wooden boxes. The newspaper helps to slow down the ripening process and checks the spread of disease. Inspect the fruit regularly and remove any which show signs of deterioration.

Crab apples can also be stored in this way for Wassail Bowl (see p. 220).

Small amounts of apples can be stored in polythene bags, provided some holes are made in each bag to prevent condensation. These should also be checked frequently.

Some dessert varieties which keep especially well are Allington Pippin, Ashmead's Kernel, Blenheim Orange, Cox's Orange Pippin, Crispin, D'Arcy Spice, Idared, Laxton's Superb, Orléans Reinette, Rosemary Russet and Spartan. Among the cookers, Bramley's Seedling, Lane's Prince Albert and Newton Wonder have a shelf-life of about six months.

THE RECIPES

Apple Purée
A Basic Recipe

In a large number of the following recipes, the apples must first be made into a purée. To avoid tiresome and space-consuming repetition, this basic recipe is given here. One pound (450 g) of apples will give about ½ pint (275 ml) of purée – this quantity is referred to in the recipes as 1 lb (450 g) apple purée.

1 LB (450 G) COOKING APPLES
GRATED RIND AND JUICE OF ½ LEMON
2 TBSP SUGAR

Peel, core and slice the apples into a pan. Add 1 tbsp water, lemon rind and juice, cover the pan and cook gently for about 10 minutes, stirring occasionally to prevent sticking. Add the sugar and beat to a purée with a wooden spoon.

If you have a microwave oven, the apples will take 4 minutes to cook.

Note

All the eggs used in these recipes are size 4.
All spoon measures are level.

4

Breakfast Dishes

Apples were they with which we were beguiled,
Yet sin, not apples, hath our souls defiled.
Apples forbid, if eat, corrupts the blood:
To eat such, when commanded, does us good.
Drink of His flagons then, thou Church, His dove,
And eat His apples, who art sick of love.

JOHN BUNYAN,
The Pilgrim's Progress

Apple cutting, from a sixteenth-century recipe book

he British breakfast is the aristocrat of early-morning meals. In its Victorian and Edwardian heyday it was a splendid spectacle: a long sideboard bearing an array of gleaming silver entrée dishes containing egg and fish dishes, devilled kidneys, bacon and sausages. Then there would be cold joints, game pies, fruit, porridge, rolls, muffins and toast, washed down with tea, coffee or chocolate. Well might Somerset Maugham remark that the best way to eat well in England was to have breakfast three times a day.

Despite its decline from such lavish magnificence, the traditional breakfast menu survives respectably in hotels and restaurants, and in many British homes, especially on Sundays. Beside it, the continental breakfast seems dull and insubstantial, yet the appeal of a light flaky croissant or a warm crisp *Brötchen* accompanied by fresh coffee is irresistible. Another delightful import from Europe is muesli, first introduced as a health dish at the Bircher-Benner clinic. Commercial presentation sometimes reduces muesli to a dusty blend of oats and dried fruit, but the original was intended to be a kind of fruit porridge. All the muesli recipes in this chapter are German and include its essential ingredients. Unpeeled apples are ideal for this satisfying high-fibre dish.

As for savoury courses, apples make an excellent substitute for eggs and contain no cholesterol.

Elsa's Muesli

Elsa was cook and housekeeper to a family in Cologne who showed me a great deal of hospitality and kindness. Her muesli was the first and the best I ever tasted.

I TBSP HONEY

4 OZ (100 G) JUMBO OATS

JUICE OF ½ LEMON

I LARGE DESSERT APPLE

Warm the honey and stir into the oats, with the lemon juice and ¼ pt (150 ml) water. Leave it for at least 15 minutes. (It can be left overnight.) Just before serving, grate an unpeeled apple into the mixture (using the coarse face of the grater), and stir it in quickly to prevent discoloration.

Apple
and Hazelnut Muesli

This is a coarser-textured muesli. Do not chop the nuts too finely.

2 TSP CLEAR HONEY	4 OZ (100 G) JUMBO OR
¼ PT (150 ML) MILK	ROLLED OATS
2 OZ (50 G) HAZELNUTS	1 TBSP LEMON JUICE
1 DESSERT APPLE	GRATED CHOCOLATE
1 BEATEN EGG	

Warm the honey and stir into the milk. Chop the hazelnuts roughly and soak them in the milk for about 15 minutes. Grate the unpeeled apple into the mixture, add the egg and oats and stir thoroughly. Add lemon juice to taste and sprinkle with grated chocolate.

Muesli with Yoghurt

4 OZ (100 G) JUMBO OATS	¼ PT (150 ML) NATURAL
2 OZ (50 G) SULTANAS	YOGHURT
¼ PT (150 ML) MILK	2 CHOPPED APPLES
3 TBSP BLACKCURRANT	1 BANANA
SYRUP	

Measure the oats and sultanas into a bowl, and add the milk, blackcurrant syrup and yoghurt. Leave overnight. Just before serving, stir in the chopped apples and the sliced banana. Other fresh fruits or nuts may be added.

Millet
and Apple Fluff

If you cannot get millet, substitute jumbo oats and turn this recipe into a muesli.

4 OZ (100 G) MILLET
2 EGGS
2 TBSP CLEAR HONEY
¼ PT (150 ML) NATURAL YOGHURT
2 DESSERT APPLES

Simmer the millet in ½ pt (275 ml) water for about 15 minutes, or until all the liquid has been absorbed. Separate the eggs. Whisk the yolks with the honey and yoghurt, then grate in the unpeeled apples and stir in the millet. When thoroughly combined, whisk the egg whites till stiff and fold in.

Apple
and Yoghurt Crisp

A satisfying breakfast dish for weight watchers.

1 DESSERT APPLE
1 ORANGE OR SATSUMA
1 TBSP CLEAR HONEY
¼ PT (150 ML) NATURAL YOGHURT
3 TBSP CORNFLAKES

Core and slice the apple. Peel the orange or satsuma and separate it into segments. Stir the honey into the yoghurt and mix with the fruit. Top with the cornflakes and serve immediately.

As round as an apple
As deep as a cup
And all the king's horses
Cannot pull it up.

Opie, *The Oxford Book of Nursery Rhymes*

Solution: a well

5
Soups and Starters

To satisfy the sharp desire I had
Of tasting those fair apples, I resolv'd
Not to defer; hunger and thirst at once,
Powerful persuaders, quicken'd at the scent
Of that alluring fruit, urg'd me so keen.

JOHN MILTON,
Paradise Lost

o the British palate, soup seems an unlikely medium for apples. Most of our well-known soups are meat- or vegetable-based, many of them constituting a substantial meal in themselves, especially in the case of broths, broses and cawls. Sometimes they used to serve the dual function of cooking the main course and providing a starter in which all the nourishing juices were retained. The original meaning of the word 'pottage' implied a dish of boiled meat and vegetables.

Fruit soups, however, have always been popular in Germany, Scandinavia and Eastern Europe. These sweet, thin fruit purées would be served cold as a starter in summer or warmed in autumn and winter, the fruit also varying according to the season. In addition, German cookery includes a wide range of soups in which fruit and vegetables combine, imparting a refreshing sharpness to the overall effect.

Apple and Almond Cream Soup

Freshly ground almonds give the best flavour. If bought ground almonds are used, make sure they are fresh and dry.

1 SMALL ONION	2 OZ (50 G) GROUND
2 STICKS CELERY	ALMONDS
½ OZ (10 G) BUTTER	SALT AND PEPPER
2 PT (1.1 L) HOT CHICKEN	1–2 TBSP DOUBLE CREAM
STOCK	CHOPPED PARSLEY
1 LB (450 G) COOKING APPLES	

Chop the onion and celery and cook gently in the butter until soft. Pour in the hot stock. Peel, core and slice the apples, and add to the stock along with the ground almonds. Bring to the boil; lower the heat, cover the pan and simmer for about an hour. At the end of the cooking time liquidize the soup, season with salt and pepper and stir in the cream. Return the pan to the stove and reheat the soup but do not let it boil. Sprinkle each serving with a little chopped parsley.

Heaven and Earth:
German Apple and Potato Soup

A thickened version of this is often served as an accompaniment to black pudding, *Wurst*, cold meat, sausages or fried liver.

3 LB (1.4 KG) POTATOES	1 TBSP WINE VINEGAR
1 LB (450 G) COOKING APPLES	4 OZ (100 G) BACON
2 PT (1.1 L) CHICKEN STOCK	2 ONIONS
1 TBSP SUGAR	FAT FOR FRYING

Dice the potatoes, peel, core and dice the apples and put them in the stock. Add the sugar and the vinegar. Bring to the boil and cook gently for 45 minutes. Purée some, but not all, of the soup, so that some of the apple and potato cubes remain. Chop the bacon and onions and fry till crisp and brown; sprinkle them over the soup just before serving.

Apple and Vegetable
Broth

(PLUCKTE FINKEN)

Like many German soups, this Bremen speciality has a misleading title: not 'plucked finches', but a thick broth of apples, beans, carrots and potatoes – an excellent winter warmer.

½ LB (225 G) WHITE HARICOT BEANS	2 CLOVES
2 BAY LEAVES	1 LARGE ONION
	1 LB (450 G) CARROTS

1 LB (450 G) POTATOES
2 COOKING APPLES
2 CHICKEN STOCK CUBES
SALT AND PEPPER

1 TBSP SUGAR
1 TBSP VINEGAR
6 OZ (175 G) STREAKY BACON

Soak the beans overnight in 3 pt (1.7 l) water. The next day, add the bay leaves, cloves and the peeled chopped onion and cook gently for 1 hour. Peel and finely dice the carrots, potatoes and apples and add to the pan. Crumble in the stock cubes and cook for a further 20 minutes. Season with salt, pepper, sugar and vinegar. Cut the bacon into small squares and fry till crisp. Sprinkle over the soup just before serving.

Quick Apple
and Tomato Soup

1 OZ (25 G) BUTTER
2 TBSP TOMATO PURÉE
2 TBSP FLOUR
1 CLOVE OF GARLIC
SALT AND PEPPER
1½ PT (850 ML) CHICKEN
   STOCK

1 DESSERT APPLE
A KNOB OF BUTTER
A HANDFUL OF FRESH
   CHIVES
¼ PT (150 ML) DOUBLE
   CREAM

Melt the butter in a pan and stir in the tomato purée, flour, crushed garlic clove and a pinch each of salt and pepper. Stir over a gentle heat and gradually add the stock.

Peel and core the apple. Slice it into rings and fry them in the butter until golden brown.

Snip the chives finely with kitchen scissors (this is easier than chopping them). Whip the cream and stir in the chives. Dish up the soup and place an apple ring on each serving. Hand round the cream separately.

A bloom on the tree when the apples are ripe
Is a sure termination of somebody's life.
E. and M. Radford, *Encyclopaedia of Superstitions*

Green Apple Soup

1 LARGE COOKING APPLE
1½ PT (850 ML) CHICKEN STOCK
4 OZ (100 G) FRESH SPINACH
1 SMALL LETTUCE OR YOUNG CABBAGE
1 TBSP SUGAR
SALT AND PEPPER

Peel and core the apple and slice it into the stock. Bring to the boil; reduce the heat and simmer for about 10 minutes, or until the apple is soft. Meanwhile wash the spinach, tear it into small pieces and cook in a very small amount of water. Finely shred the cabbage or lettuce and add to the soup with the spinach. Cook gently for a further 20 minutes, and then liquidize the soup. Add the sugar and season to taste.

Apple
Soup with Dumplings

This can be served chilled as a summer starter, or warm in colder weather. For a more substantial dish, serve with dumplings.

1 LB (450 G) COOKING APPLES
1 STRIP LEMON PEEL
½ STICK CINNAMON
1 OZ (25 G) SEMOLINA
2 OZ (50 G) SUGAR
WHITE WINE OR CIDER TO
    TASTE

For dumplings
2 OZ (50 G) BUTTER
1 BEATEN EGG
2½ OZ (60 G) FLOUR
1 TSP MILK
PINCH OF SALT
1 TBSP SUGAR

Peel, core and slice the apples and put them in a pan with 2 pt (1.1 l) water, and the lemon peel and cinnamon. Cook gently for about ½ hour; remove the peel and cinnamon. Liquidize the apples, return to the pan and sprinkle in the semolina and sugar. Stir over a gentle heat until slightly thickened. Add a little wine or cider to taste.

For the dumplings, work the butter till soft and gradually work in the other ingredients. Form into small dumplings using a teaspoon and drop them into the hot soup. Let them cook for 3 minutes.

Smoked Mackerel and Apple Mousse

2 DESSERT APPLES
JUICE OF ½ LEMON
2 SMOKED MACKEREL FILLETS
½ PT (275 ML) SOURED
  CREAM
2 TSP GELATINE

2 EGG WHITES
SALT AND PEPPER
A LITTLE CUCUMBER OR
  CHOPPED PARSLEY TO
  DECORATE

Peel, core and slice the apples. Cook them gently in 2 tbsp water and the lemon juice till soft; drain, reserving the liquid. Mash them with the mackerel fillets, add the soured cream and liquidize. Season to taste. Soak the gelatine in the reserved liquid, and then warm it until completely dissolved, and stir into the mixture. Whisk the egg whites till stiff, fold into the mixture and pour into a soufflé dish or individual ramekins and chill. Decorate with cucumber slices or chopped parsley.

Waldorf Apples

6 CRISP DESSERT APPLES
2 STICKS CELERY
1 OZ (25 G) WALNUTS
2 TSP CHOPPED PARSLEY

1 TBSP MAYONNAISE
4 OZ (100 G) COTTAGE
  CHEESE
6 WALNUT HALVES

Core the unpeeled apples and cut a slice off the top of each one. Finely chop the celery and walnuts and mix with the chopped parsley, mayonnaise and cottage cheese. Fill the apples with this mixture, spooning any surplus over the tops. Decorate each with a walnut half.

> 'Very astonishing indeed! Strange thing!'
> (Turning the Dumpling round, rejoined the King), . . .
> 'But Goody, tell me where, where, where's the Seam?'
> 'Sir, there's no seam (quoth she): I never knew
> That folks did apple dumplings sew.' . . .
> 'No! (cried the staring Monarch with a grin)
> How, how the devil got the apple in?'
>
> Peter Pindar (John Wolcot): 'The Apple Dumplings and the King'

6
Salads, Vegetables and Sauces

To bend with apples the moss'd cottage trees
And fill all fruit with ripeness to the core.

JOHN KEATS,
'Ode to Autumn'

ne of my German cookery books quotes an unnamed French book in this concise definition of a salad: 'a combination of contrasting ingredients, their flavours subtly harmonized, blended into the most confusing mixture'. Sweet and savoury, sharp and bland, piquant and mild flavours can be tossed together in a salad, and there are endless possibilities of combinations and variations.

Apples lend themselves well to salads as their flavour teams well with meat, vegetables, cheese and yoghurt, and with other fruits; unpeeled apples add colour. It is important, however, to cover apples quickly with dressing to prevent browning; if this is not possible, they should be prepared at the last possible moment and dipped in lemon juice to keep the flesh white.

As an ingredient in hot vegetable dishes, apples may seem much less appropriate, but as with the soup recipes they can provide a delicious piquancy. Sweet-and-sour red cabbage is the traditional accompaniment to the Danish Christmas Day goose and is extremely popular throughout Germany and Eastern Europe, while Americans love the combination of apples with root vegetables, liberally sweetened with brown sugar. However illogical this may sound the results fully justify the experiment.

Apple Salad Ring

3 TSP POWDERED GELATINE
1 PT (575 ML) APPLE JUICE
2 STICKS CELERY
1 AVOCADO
2 DESSERT APPLES

1 OZ (25 G) WALNUTS OR
HAZELNUTS

To serve

SALAD DRESSING DILUTED
WITH APPLE JUICE

Soften the gelatine in one third of the apple juice. Bring the remaining juice to the boil, add to the gelatine mixture and stir till it dissolves completely. Put in the refrigerator to chill. Meanwhile, dice the celery, the avocado and the unpeeled apples. Roughly chop the nuts. When the jelly is syrupy, stir in these ingredients and pour into an oiled ring mould. Leave in the refrigerator for several hours until set. Turn out carefully on to a plate and serve with salad dressing diluted with apple juice.

Pork, Apple and Rice Salad

4 OZ (100 G) RICE	1 TBSP CHOPPED PARSLEY
8 OZ (225 G) LEFTOVER	1 TBSP LEMON JUICE
ROAST PORK	2 TBSP MAYONNAISE
2 DESSERT APPLES	SALT AND PEPPER
2 TOMATOES	

Cook the rice in boiling salted water, drain and refresh. Cube the pork and apples and slice the tomatoes. Add to the rice with the parsley. Whisk together the lemon juice and mayonnaise and season to taste. Mix into the other ingredients.

Winter Salad

1 LB (450 G) POTATOES	1 SMALL RAW BEETROOT
1 SMALL ONION	1 MEDIUM RAW CARROT
1 TSP CHOPPED PARSLEY	2 TBSP FRENCH DRESSING
1 STICK CELERY	SALT AND PEPPER
2 DESSERT APPLES	4 OZ (100 G) CHEESE
¼ WHITE CABBAGE	

Boil the potatoes and dice them. Finely chop the onion and parsley and mix with the potatoes while they are still warm. Chop the celery and apples, and shred the cabbage, beetroot and carrot finely. Put everything in a salad bowl and toss with the French dressing and seasoning. Sprinkle with grated cheese.

Herring and Apple Salad
(HERINGSALAT)

I LB (450 G) PICKLED
  HERRING
I LB (450 G) POTATOES,
  COOKED AND DICED
I SMALL BEETROOT, COOKED
  AND DICED
2 LARGE DESSERT APPLES,
  CORED AND DICED

I SMALL ONION, FINELY
  CHOPPED
¼ PT (150 ML) SOURED
  CREAM
3 TBSP FRENCH DRESSING
I TBSP LEMON JUICE
SALT
FRESHLY GROUND PEPPER

Cut the herring into bite-sized pieces and combine with the potatoes, beetroot, apples and onion. Mix together the soured cream, French dressing and lemon juice, season to taste and combine with the other ingredients.

Apple, Pasta
and Sweetcorn Salad

8 OZ (225 G) PASTA SPIRALS
4 TBSP FRENCH DRESSING
SALT AND PEPPER
2 DESSERT APPLES

I SMALL ONION
7 OZ (200 G) CAN SWEETCORN
4 OZ (100 G) BACON
CHOPPED PARSLEY

Cook the pasta in boiling salted water and drain. Stir in the French dressing and seasoning to taste. Chop the unpeeled apples roughly and the peeled onion finely. Drain the sweetcorn. Chop the bacon and fry till crisp. Combine all the ingredients and sprinkle with chopped parsley.

These are the youths that thunder at a playhouse and fight for bitten apples.

Shakespeare, *Henry VIII*

Meran Salad

6 OZ (175 G) MACARONI	6 OZ (175 G) SMOKED HAM
8 OZ (225 G) COLD COOKED POTATOES	6 OZ (175 G) CARROTS
	3 TBSP THICK MAYONNAISE
3 STICKS CELERY	¼ PT (150 ML) YOGHURT
3 CRISP DESSERT APPLES	SALT, PEPPER, SUGAR

Cook the macaroni in salted water for about 10 minutes or according to the instructions on the packet; drain, refresh and cool. Chop the potatoes, celery, apples and ham. Grate the carrots coarsely. Blend together the mayonnaise and yoghurt and add seasoning to taste. Mix all the ingredients together in a salad bowl and chill before serving.

Coleslaw

The name in Dutch means 'cabbage salad'.

½ SMALL WHITE CABBAGE	2 TBSP CIDER VINEGAR
2 MEDIUM CARROTS	4 TBSP OLIVE OIL
2 CRISP DESSERT APPLES	1 TBSP MAYONNAISE

Finely shred the cabbage, carrots and the cored apples. Whisk together the remaining ingredients and toss everything together.

Curried Coleslaw

2 DESSERT APPLES	1 OZ (25 G) RAISINS
1 OZ (25 G) CHEDDAR CHEESE	JUICE OF ½ LEMON
¼ DUTCH OR RED CABBAGE	¼ PT (150 ML) YOGHURT
1 STICK CELERY	1 TSP CURRY POWDER
2 OZ (50 G) MUSHROOMS	

Grate the apples and cheese. Shred the cabbage. Slice the celery and mushrooms. Combine in a salad bowl with the raisins. Blend together the lemon juice, yoghurt and curry powder. Pour over the salad and toss.

Red Coleslaw

½ RED CABBAGE
2 RED DESSERT APPLES
2 OZ (50 G) WALNUTS
2 TBSP BROWN SUGAR
SALT AND PEPPER

2 TBSP CIDER VINEGAR
½ TSP DRY MUSTARD
¼ PT (150 ML) SOURED
CREAM

Shred the cabbage and grate the unpeeled apples. Chop the walnuts coarsely. Put them all in a salad bowl. Whisk together the remaining ingredients, pour into the bowl and toss thoroughly.

Crunchy Apple and Avocado Salad

2 GREEN DESSERT APPLES
2 RED DESSERT APPLES
1 AVOCADO
2 OZ (50 G) HAZELNUTS

4 OZ (100 G) BEAN SPROUTS
1 BUNCH OF CRESS
4–6 TBSP FRENCH DRESSING

Core and chop the unpeeled apples; peel, stone and chop the avocado. Chop the hazelnuts roughly. Mix all the ingredients and toss well.

And pluck till time and times are done
The silver apples of the moon
The golden apples of the sun.
W. B. Yeats, 'The Song of Wandering Aengus'

66

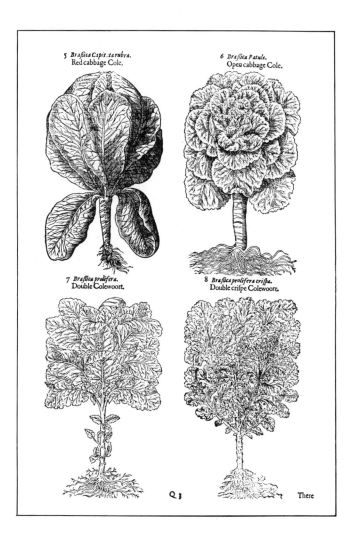

5 *Braſica Capit:ta rubra.*
Red cabbage Cole.

6 *Braſica Patula.*
Open cabbage Cole.

7 *Braſica prolifera.*
Double Colewoort.

8 *Braſica prolifera criſpa.*
Double criſpe Colewoort.

Q 3

There

67

Dutch Cheese and Apple Salad

2 CRISP DESSERT APPLES	6 TBSP OLIVE OIL
6 OZ (175 G) GOUDA CHEESE	4 TBSP VINEGAR
6 OZ (175 G) HAM	I TSP DRY MUSTARD
3 SPRING ONIONS	PINCH OF SALT

Core and slice the apples. De-rind the cheese and cut it into strips. Cut the ham in strips and chop the onions finely. Put all these ingredients into a salad bowl. Put the oil, vinegar, mustard and salt into a screw-top jar and shake vigorously till well blended. Pour over the salad and toss.

Prawn and Apple Salad

2 DESSERT APPLES	6 OZ (175 G) PEELED PRAWNS
JUICE OF I LEMON	8 OZ (225 G) COTTAGE
2 TSP WINE VINEGAR	CHEESE
I SMALL GREEN PEPPER	2 TBSP MAYONNAISE
I SMALL YELLOW PEPPER	LETTUCE LEAVES
2 STICKS CELERY	

Dice the apples and toss in the lemon juice and vinegar. Slice the peppers and celery and add to the apples with the prawns. Blend the cottage cheese with the mayonnaise. Arrange some lettuce leaves in a salad bowl, spoon the cheese mixture on top and cover with the prawn and apple mixture.

Sweet-and-Sour Red Cabbage

(RØDKAAL)

In Denmark this is the traditional accompaniment to the Christmas

Day goose. (It is also very good with pork or duck.) It can be reheated in a moderate oven or in a pan over a low heat without spoiling.

I SMALL RED CABBAGE	2 TBSP BROWN SUGAR
2 OZ (50 G) BUTTER	I TBSP VINEGAR
I SMALL ONION	SALT AND PEPPER
I LARGE COOKING APPLE	

Remove the stalk from the cabbage and shred the leaves finely. Melt the butter in a large saucepan. Chop the onion and cook gently in the butter till soft but not brown. Add the cabbage gradually and mix well to coat it with the butter. Now add the peeled, sliced apple, the brown sugar and the vinegar. Mix well, cover the saucepan and cook over a very low heat for about 45 minutes, stirring occasionally. Season to taste.

Apple, Parsnip and Walnut Soufflé

This is a good accompaniment to roast game and poultry.

2 LB (I KG) PARSNIPS	2 OZ (50 G) CHOPPED
UNSWEETENED APPLE PURÉE	WALNUTS
MADE FROM I LB (450 G)	2 TBSP SINGLE CREAM
APPLES (p. 43)	2 TBSP PORT
I TBSP BROWN SUGAR	3 EGGS
	SALT AND PEPPER

Butter a large soufflé dish. Peel the parsnips, cook in boiling salted water till soft and purée or liquidize. Blend in the apple purée, brown sugar, walnuts, cream, port and egg yolks and beat till smooth. Season to taste with salt and pepper. Whisk the egg whites till stiff and fold them into the mixture. Pour into the buttered soufflé dish and bake at 400°F (200°C, Mark 6) for 25 minutes.

Canadian Swede and Apple Casserole

2 FIRM DESSERT APPLES
1 LB (450 G) SWEDE
SALT AND PEPPER
2 OZ (50 G) BROWN SUGAR
1½ OZ (40 G) BUTTER

Peel, core and dice the apples. Peel and dice the swede and toss with the apples, salt, pepper and sugar. Put everything in a small casserole or baking dish and dot with butter. Cover and bake at 350°F (180°C, Mark 4) for 1 hour.

Sweet Potato and Apple

This is a Creole dish, popular in the southern United States. It makes an unusual accompaniment to cold roast meat.

2 LB (1 KG) SWEET POTATOES
3 OZ (75 G) MOLASSES OR TREACLE
6 OZ (175 G) BUTTER
1 LB (450 G) DESSERT APPLES
1 TSP SALT

Peel and cube the sweet potatoes and cook them in boiling salted water for about 25 minutes. Meanwhile, warm the molasses with half the butter. Peel, core and slice the apples and turn them in this mixture till they are well coated. Let them cook gently for 10 minutes. Drain the potatoes and mash them with the remaining butter and the salt. Spread a layer of the mashed potato in a buttered ovenproof dish, cover with a layer of apples and repeat this until the ingredients are used up. Bake at 350°F (180°C, Mark 4) for 20 minutes.

Apple
and Horseradish Cream

Try this Austrian relish with roast beef for a change. If you cannot get fresh horseradish, use ready-made horseradish sauce.

¼ PT (150 ML) DOUBLE CREAM
2 TSP GRATED HORSERADISH
1 DESSERT APPLE, PEELED AND GRATED
½ TSP SUGAR
PINCH OF SALT

Whip the cream and fold in the horseradish and apple. Add the sugar and salt to taste.

Spread Apple Sauce

This may be served hot or cold with roast pork or duck. It becomes firmer as it cools.

1 LB (450 G) COOKING APPLES
2 CLOVES
1 TBSP CIDER VINEGAR
2 OZ (50 G) SUGAR
½ OZ (10 G) BUTTER

Core and quarter the unpeeled apples. Cook in ¼ pt (150 ml) boiling water with the cloves and vinegar in a pan with a close-fitting lid until tender. Sieve. Return to the heat and stir in the sugar and butter.

7
Snacks and Supper Dishes

Eat an apple before going to bed,
Make the doctor beg his bread.

ANON

lthough the apple is not as nutritious as some fruits, certain life-giving properties have been attributed to it in legend. The magic apples of Idunn allowed the Norse gods to retain their youth and one of these fruits, sent by Frigga to King Rerir, cured his wife of infertility. In Arabian mythology, Prince Ahmed's apple cured every known disorder and even restored his sweetheart to life.

Sadly, such powers are beyond the scope of ordinary apples! They are, however, rich in fibre and raw apples promote healthy teeth and gums. Malic acid is soothing to the stomach and combats mild indigestion, bearing out the statement of Brillat-Savarin that an apple at bedtime induces sleep. John Gerarde, in his *Herbal* of 1597, states that 'Apples be good for an hot stomache; those that are austere or somewhat harsh do strengthen a weak or feeble stomache proceeding of heate.'

The following recipes are all quickly prepared and are suitable as light lunch or supper dishes. A green salad and crusty bread as accompaniments will provide a substantial meal.

Macaroni Savoury

2 OZ (50 G) MACARONI	2 OZ (50 G) BUTTER
1 LARGE COOKING APPLE	2 OZ (50 G) FLOUR
1 SMALL ONION	½ PT (275 ML) MILK
1 TBSP OIL	4 OZ (100 G) GRATED CHEESE
1 TBSP TOMATO PURÉE	

Cook the macaroni in lightly salted boiling water. Meanwhile, chop the apple and onion finely, fry them gently in the oil till soft, add the tomato purée and cook for 1 minute. Drain the macaroni and mix it in. In another pan, melt the butter, stir in the flour and gradually add the milk, stirring constantly. When the sauce is smooth beat in the cheese. Turn the macaroni mixture into a small ovenproof dish, pour over the sauce and bake at 350°F (180°C, Mark 4) for 30 minutes.

Apple Galette
with Black Pudding
(GALETTE DE POMMES AUX BOUDINS)

6 FIRM DESSERT APPLES	12 OZ (350 G) GARLIC
2 OZ (50 G) BUTTER	SAUSAGE
SALT AND PEPPER	2 TBSP OIL
12 OZ (350 G) BLACK	I TBSP CALVADOS
PUDDING	(OPTIONAL)

Peel, core and slice the apples. Melt the butter in a heavy frying-pan, sprinkle the apple slices with salt and pepper and arrange them in the pan. Cook over a brisk heat till golden; turn them, cover the pan and leave to cook on a low heat for 15 minutes. They should be soft but unbroken. Meanwhile, prick the black pudding and garlic sausage to prevent bursting and cut each into four pieces. Cook them in oil in another frying-pan, briskly at first and then over a low heat for 5 minutes. Turn the apple cake out on to a hot plate and arrange alternate slices of black pudding and sausage over it. Sprinkle with calvados, if using, and serve immediately.

Kent, sir – everyone knows Kent – apples, cherries, hops and women.
Dickens, *The Pickwick Papers*

Savoury Baked Apples

I OZ (25 G) BUTTER	I TBSP SEASONED FLOUR
8 OZ (225 G) MINCED PORK	I BEATEN EGG
SALT AND PEPPER	I OZ (25 G) BREADCRUMBS
4–6 LARGE COOKING APPLES	

Melt the butter and fry the mince till brown. Season it well. Peel and core the apples, roll them in the flour, the beaten egg and the breadcrumbs. Stand them in a baking dish and fill the centres with the mince. Bake at 375°F (190°C, Mark 5) for half an hour.

Bacon Cakes

12 OZ (350 G) STREAKY BACON	1 TBSP FLOUR
1 SMALL ONION	1 TBSP NATURAL BRAN
1 MEDIUM COOKING APPLE	PINCH OF MIXED HERBS
1 LARGE POTATO	BLACK PEPPER
1 EGG, BEATEN	HOT OIL FOR FRYING

These can be made very easily by putting all the ingredients except the oil in a food processor and working them to a smooth paste. Alternatively, mince the bacon, grate the onion, apple and potato, and combine thoroughly. Blend in the beaten egg, flour, bran, herbs and pepper.

Heat the oil in a frying-pan and drop in large spoonfuls of the mixture. Fry for 10 minutes on each side till crisp.

Apple
and Bacon Frazes

A fraze is a thick light pancake, popular in the eighteenth century. This recipe makes four.

Filling	*Batter*
3 RASHERS BACON	4 EGGS
OIL OR BUTTER FOR FRYING	¼ PT (150 ML) CREAMY MILK
2 DESSERT APPLES	2 OZ (50 G) FLOUR
	1 TBSP SHERRY
	1 OZ (25 G) MELTED BUTTER
	PINCH OF SALT
	PINCH OF GRATED NUTMEG

Chop the bacon and fry it until the fat runs. Core and slice the apples and fry with the bacon until lightly browned. Set aside and keep warm. Separate the eggs and beat the yolks with the other batter ingredients. Whip the whites until stiff and fold into the batter. Melt some butter or oil in a pancake or omelette pan, pour in a little batter and fry until the underside is firm. Lay some apple and bacon on top, pour on a little more batter and cook gently until the top surface becomes firm. Turn the fraze carefully and cook the other side. Continue in this way until all the ingredients are used up.

Apples and Bacon
(AEBLEFLAESK)

In Denmark this is served with rye bread as a light lunch or supper dish but it is also excellent for breakfast.

20 RASHERS OF BACON
2–4 TART DESSERT APPLES
SUGAR TO TASTE
RYE OR WHOLEMEAL BREAD

Fry the bacon until crisp, remove from the pan and keep warm. Core the apples, slice into rings and fry in the bacon fat until soft. Add sugar to taste.

Arrange the apples in a shallow dish topped with the bacon and serve with plenty of rye or wholemeal bread.

Cheesy
Apple Bacon Fritters

These can be served with sausages, bacon, fried tomatoes, mushrooms or toast. You can use leftover cooked meat instead of bacon.

4 OZ (100 G) PLAIN FLOUR   1 TSP DRIED MUSTARD
PINCH OF SALT   4 OZ (100 G) GRATED CHEESE

I EGG	FAT FOR FRYING
½ PT (275 ML) MILK	2 SHARP-FLAVOURED
4 OZ (100 G) BACON	DESSERT APPLES

Sift together the dry ingredients and add the cheese. Make a well in the centre, add the egg yolk and a little milk. Beat till smooth, gradually adding the remaining milk. Whisk the egg white till stiff and fold it in.

Chop the bacon. Fry it for a few minutes until crisp. Peel, core and grate the apples. Add both to the batter. Heat the fat and test it by dropping in a small piece of bread. If it sizzles and turns golden brown the temperature is right. Drop spoonfuls of the batter into the fat and fry till golden on both sides.

Apple Rarebit

4 OZ (100 G) CHEESE, GRATED	I DESSERT APPLE, GRATED
I TBSP BEER	½ OZ (10 G) BUTTER
I TSP DRIED MUSTARD	4 SLICES TOAST
SALT AND PEPPER	

Put the cheese and beer into a pan. Stir over a low heat until the cheese melts. Add the seasoning, apple and butter, and stir till well blended. Spread the mixture on the toast and grill until bubbling and golden brown.

Ham and Apple Pancakes

(FICELLE NORMANDE)

Batter	Filling
4 OZ (100 G) PLAIN FLOUR	4 DESSERT APPLES
2 EGGS	8 OZ (225 G) HAM
I DESSERTSPOON OLIVE OIL	SALT AND PEPPER
½ PT (275 ML) MILK	¼ PT (150 ML) DOUBLE
2 OZ (50 G) MELTED BUTTER	CREAM
A LITTLE EXTRA BUTTER	4 OZ (100 G) GRUYÈRE CHEESE

First make the pancake batter. Sift the flour into a bowl, make a well in it and add the eggs and oil. Beat until all the flour is absorbed. Gradually add the milk, beating constantly; then beat in the melted butter. Set aside while you prepare the filling.

Peel, core and grate the apples and chop the ham. Mix together and season with salt and pepper.

Melt the extra butter in a pancake or omelette pan. Pour in enough batter to cover the bottom. Cook till firm underneath, and then flip over and cook the other side. Slide the pancake on to a plate and put a portion of filling on it. Roll it up and put it in a serving dish. Prepare the remaining pancakes in the same way.

Pour the cream over the pancakes and sprinkle with the grated cheese. Bake for 10 minutes at 350°F (180°C, Mark 4) and serve immediately.

Carentan Sausages

(ANDOUILLETTES À LA MODE DE CARENTAN)

These are mustard-coated sausages served on a bed of buttered apples. Make sure you use a mild French mustard.

2 TBSP FRENCH MUSTARD
4 OZ (100 G) BUTTER
1 LB (450 G) PORK SAUSAGES
4 DESSERT APPLES
JUICE OF ½ LEMON
SALT AND PEPPER

Blend the mustard with half the butter. Cut the sausages in half lengthwise and spread with this mixture. Peel and core the apples and slice them into rounds. Sprinkle with the lemon juice and cook in the remaining butter till soft. Season and arrange the apples in an ovenproof dish. Arrange the sausages on top. Cook for 20 minutes at 400°F (200°C, Mark 6). Serve at once with plenty of crusty French bread to mop up the juices.

Stolen sweets are always sweeter,
Stolen kisses much completer,
Stolen looks are nice in chapels,
Stolen, stolen, be your apples!
Leigh Hunt, 'Song of Fairies Robbing an Orchard'

8
Main Course Dishes

O where are you going to, all you big steamers
With England's own coal, up and down the salt seas?
We are going to fetch you your bread and your butter,
Your beef, pork and mutton, eggs, apples and cheese.

JOHN MASEFIELD

sharp-flavoured apple sauce is the traditional accompaniment to roast pork, especially for an English Sunday lunch, but this is by no means the only meat dish to include apples, or indeed the only way in which apples can complement the flavour of pork. In his book *The Accomplish'd Cook* (1665), Robert May gives this recipe:

To Broil Ghines of Pork: Broil them as you do the rack but bread them and serve them with vinegar and pepper. Or sometimes apples in slices, boil'd in beer and beaten with butter to a mash.

In medieval times sweet and savoury foods were combined much more frequently than today. *The Form of Cury* is a recipe collection compiled in 1390 in which we find apples featuring in savoury recipes with the most unlikely ingredients. Take, for example, Lenten tart with a filling of salmon, codlings, prunes and damsons, or the combination of apples, water parsnips, batter, ale, saffron and almond milk for an unusual fritter recipe. By Elizabethan times a combination of pippins, chopped hard-boiled eggs, currants, raisins, sugar, orange and lemon rind and spices had become a popular stuffing or pie filling. These strange mixtures may have owed their origin to the crusaders as they are reminiscent of Middle Eastern cuisine. One finds echoes of them also in some of the savoury pies mentioned in the introduction to Chapter 9.

In this chapter I have tried to assemble as varied an assortment as possible to demonstrate the versatility of apples with meat, fish, pasta, pulses and cheese.

> **Art thou the topmost apple**
> **The gatherers could reach**
> **Reddening on the bough?**
> **Shall I not take thee?**
> Sappho, *Odes*

Poulet d'Orléans

This is named after the Île d'Orléans in the St Lawrence river, where apples are plentiful.

3 LB (1.4 KG) CHICKEN
SALT
2 OZ (50 G) BROWN RICE
1 STICK CELERY
3 DESSERT APPLES
1 OZ (25 G) RAISINS

1 OZ (25 G) MELTED BUTTER
PINCH OF THYME
FAT FOR FRYING
4 RASHERS BACON
¼ PT (150 ML) CREAM
1 TBSP BRANDY

Wipe the chicken inside and rub with salt. Cook the rice and mix with the chopped celery, one chopped apple, raisins, melted butter and thyme. Stuff the chicken with this mixture and truss. Brown the chicken in the fat and then remove it from the fat. Core and slice the two remaining apples and fry the slices. Put some in the bottom of a casserole, lay the chicken on top and cover the breast with bacon. Tuck the rest of the apple down the sides.

Cover and bake at 350°F (180°C, Mark 4) for 2 hours. Remove the lid during the last 15 minutes to brown the chicken. Pour in the cream and brandy and reheat gently. Cut the chicken into portions and arrange on a serving dish. Pour over a little of the sauce and hand the rest round separately.

Roast Duck
with Apple Stuffing

(CANARD AUX POMMES)

1 DUCK, ABOUT 4 LB (1.8 KG)
SALT
4 OZ (100 G) BREADCRUMBS
1 LB (450 G) APPLE PURÉE
 (p. 43)
PINCH OF CINNAMON
PINCH OF NUTMEG

2 OZ (50 G) BUTTER
3 TBSP WINE VINEGAR
1 TSP CASTER SUGAR
FRESHLY GROUND PEPPER
1 TBSP APPLE JELLY
A LITTLE CIDER

Prick the skin of the duck with a fork and rub it with salt. Mix the breadcrumbs with the apple purée and flavour with cinnamon and nutmeg. Stuff the duck with this mixture and sew up the opening, or plug it with kitchen foil. Place it on a rack over a roasting tin and roast at 400°F (200°C, Mark 6) for 30 minutes per pound.

Melt the butter in a saucepan, add the vinegar, sugar and pepper. Bring to the boil and use to baste the duck after about 15 minutes' cooking. Baste it frequently during the cooking period, and empty the tin if too much fat accumulates.

When the cooking is completed, pour off the fat and stir the apple jelly into the juices. Deglaze the pan with a little cider and serve this sauce with the duck.

Breast of Duck with Apples and Raisins

4 DUCK BREASTS	4 OZ (100 G) RAISINS
SALT AND PEPPER	¼ PT (150 ML) WHITE WINE
1 TSP DRIED MARJORAM	2–3 TBSP BRANDY
8 OZ (225 G) DESSERT APPLES	

Rub the duck pieces with salt, pepper and marjoram. Peel, core and thickly slice the apples. Wash and drain the raisins. Put the duck, apples and raisins into a casserole, pour over the wine, cover and cook at 350°F (180°C, Mark 4) for about 2 hours.

To serve, arrange the duck pieces on a serving dish and keep warm. Remove the apples and raisins from the casserole with a perforated spoon, put them in a pan with the brandy and warm through. Spoon over the duck.

Skim the gravy, check its seasoning and serve separately.

The flavour of roast goose is complemented by an apple stuffing or accompaniment. A traditional Bavarian method is to stuff the goose with small whole apples, unpeeled. The following two recipes are further examples of this combination.

Danish Roast Goose

(GAANSESTEG MED AEBLER OG SVEDSKER)

This is traditional Christmas fare in Denmark.

1 GOOSE	A SPRIG OF ROSEMARY
SALT AND PEPPER	(OR ½ TSP DRIED)
8 OZ (225 G) ONIONS	4 OZ (100 G) BREADCRUMBS
8 OZ (225 G) APPLES	¼ PT (150 ML) BEER
2 OZ (50 G) BUTTER	1 TBSP FLOUR
12 PRUNES, SOAKED	
OVERNIGHT	

Wipe the goose, rub inside and outside with salt and prick the skin all over with a fork.

To make the stuffing, chop the onions and apples finely and fry in the butter till soft. Stone and chop the prunes, crush the rosemary and add to the pan with the breadcrumbs and seasoning. Stuff the goose with this mixture and sew it up or skewer it firmly. Place it on a rack in a roasting tin, pour over a little water and roast at 350°F (180°C, Mark 4) for 15 minutes per pound, basting occasionally.

When cooked, remove the goose from the oven and keep it warm. Pour off the fat and stir the flour and then the beer into the remaining juices. Bring this mixture to the boil and serve with the goose. Serve with Sweet-and-Sour Red Cabbage (p. 68) and small boiled potatoes tossed in a light caramel sauce made from butter and sugar.

Ontario Roast Goose
with Apple and Sage Stuffing

I GOOSE	I TSP DRIED SAGE
SALT	¼ TSP BLACK PEPPER
8 OZ (225 G) COOKING APPLES	¼ TSP GROUND CLOVES
6 OZ (175 G) WHOLEMEAL	¼ TSP CINNAMON
BREADCRUMBS	

Prepare the goose as in the previous recipe. Peel, core and roughly chop the apples, combine with the other stuffing ingredients and stuff the body cavity of the goose three quarters full. Sew or skewer it firmly and roast as above.

Serve with Canadian Swede and Apple Casserole (p. 70) and roast potatoes.

The following two pheasant recipes are specialties of Normandy, using the local products: apples, calvados and cream.

Pheasant
Vallée d'Auge

This should be served on a plate surrounded by a selection of fresh vegetables, e.g. baby carrots, peas and French beans.

2 CARROTS

2 ONIONS

2 OZ (50 G) BUTTER

2 HEN PHEASANTS, PLUCKED
   AND DRAWN

SALT AND PEPPER

½ PT (275 ML) JELLIED STOCK

2 TBSP CALVADOS

¼ PT (150 ML) DOUBLE
   CREAM

2–4 FIRM DESSERT APPLES

Chop the vegetables and cook them gently in 1 oz (25 g) butter in a large ovenproof pan until they are soft but not brown. Add the pheasants to the pan and brown quickly. Season them with salt and pepper, baste with the melted butter and put them in a hot oven (400°F, 200°C, Mark 6) for 15–20 minutes. Take out and skim off any excess fat. Pour the stock round the pheasants and pour the calvados over them. Reduce the oven temperature to 350°F (180°C, Mark 4) and cover the pheasants with foil. Cook for 1 hour, removing the foil after 45 minutes. Take up the pheasants, carve and keep them warm. Skim and sieve the sauce, add the cream and reheat but do not let it boil.

Peel and core the apples and cut them into thick rings. Fry gently in the rest of the butter until golden but not brown. Serve up the pheasant on the fried apples, surrounded by a selection of vegetables and hand the sauce round separately.

Pheasant with Apple
and Cream-cheese Stuffing

(FAISAN À LA CAUCHOISE)

1 PHEASANT, PLUCKED AND
   DRAWN

3 OZ (75 G) BUTTER

6 FIRM DESSERT APPLES
   (PREFERABLY COX'S)

3 SMALL CREAM CHEESES
   (e.g. PETITS SUISSES)

SALT AND PEPPER

1 TBSP CALVADOS

½ PT (275 ML) DOUBLE
   CREAM

To serve

2 BUNCHES OF WATERCRESS

Set the oven to 350°F (180°C, Mark 4). Melt half the butter and brown the pheasant evenly in it. Peel and core two apples, and grate or chop them finely. Work them into the cheese, season well, and stuff the pheasant with this mixture. Sew up the opening or plug it with crumpled foil. Butter an ovenproof casserole. Peel, core and slice the remaining apples and arrange half of them in the casserole. Lay the pheasant on top and tuck the remaining slices of apple down the sides. Warm the calvados and pour it over the bird. Cook for 1 hour; stir the cream into the sauce and return to the oven for 25 minutes.

Take up the pheasant, carve it and arrange on an oval serving dish. Arrange the apple slices down each side and garnish each end with a bunch of watercress.

You can cook partridge in the same way, omitting the stuffing. Use a brace of partridge, but after browning cut each bird in half lengthways. Cook for 30 minutes, along with 2 large apples, peeled, cored and sliced, and a liqueur glass of calvados. When the cooking time is completed, stir in 2 tbsp cream and reheat.

Filet de Boeuf Saint Amand

This is an impressive dinner-party dish. It is expensive, but quick and easy to prepare and there is no waste.

1 TBSP OIL	1 OZ (25 G) BUTTER
1 TBSP BUTTER	1 WINEGLASS CALVADOS
2½–3 LB (1.1–1.4 KG) FILLET	¼ PT (150 ML) CREAM
OF BEEF	
6 OZ (175 G) SLICED	*To serve*
MUSHROOMS	2 BUNCHES WATERCRESS
4 DESSERT APPLES	GAME CHIPS

Set the oven to 400°F (200°C, Mark 6). Put the oil and butter in a roasting tin and place in the oven till hot. Then remove it from the oven, put in the meat and baste it thoroughly. Set the meat on a grid in the tin and return to the oven. Cook for 15 minutes per pound (450 g) plus 15 minutes over, basting every 15 minutes and turning the meat at the half-way stage. Ten minutes before the cooking time is completed, add the mushrooms to the tin below the meat.

Meanwhile peel, core and slice the apples and fry in the butter. When the cooking is completed, take out the meat and mushrooms and keep warm. Warm the calvados, set it alight and pour it, flaming, over the meat. Deglaze the roasting tin with the cream. Stir in the mushrooms.

Carve the beef and arrange on a serving dish surrounded by the fried apple slices and the game chips. Pour over the cream and mushrooms. Place a bunch of watercress at each end of the serving dish.

Roast Stuffed
Loin of Pork Dijonnaise

4½ LB (2 KG) LOIN OF PORK 1 MEDIUM APPLE
1 SMALL ONION 4 OZ (100 G) BREADCRUMBS

PINCH OF SALT	3 TBSP MILK
1 TSP DRIED SAGE (OR 2 TSP	2 TSP FRENCH MUSTARD
FRESH SAGE)	1 TBSP FLOUR

Ask your butcher to remove the bone from the meat. Chop the onion and apple finely, and combine with 3 oz (75 g) breadcrumbs, salt, sage and milk. Spread this stuffing over the meat, roll up and tie securely. Spread the skin of the pork with mustard and pat on the remaining breadcrumbs.

Put the meat on a rack in a roasting tin and pour in 1 pt (575 ml) water. Roast at 325°F (170°C, Mark 3) for at least 2 hours.

Another way of preparing this roast is to ask the butcher to crack the bones; then cut deep pockets in the meat and press some stuffing into each.

To serve, carve the pork in slices, arrange on a serving dish and keep warm. Pour off the fat from the roasting tin and stir the flour into the juices to make gravy. Pour some over the meat and hand the rest round in a sauceboat.

Roast Tenderloin with Apple and Prune Stuffing

(MØRBRAD MED SVEDSKER OG AEBLER)

4 PORK TENDERLOINS	4 OZ (100 G) BREADCRUMBS
4 OZ (100 G) BUTTER	½ TSP DRIED ROSEMARY
8 OZ (225 G) COOKING APPLES	SALT AND PEPPER
8 OZ (225 G) ONIONS	¼ PT (150 ML) WHITE WINE
12 PRUNES, SOAKED	¼ PT (150 ML) DOUBLE
OVERNIGHT	CREAM

To prepare the tenderloins, with a sharp knife make a cut lengthwise down the middle of each tenderloin, about two thirds of the way through. Open them out, cover with wet greaseproof paper and beat flat with a meat tenderizer or a small heavy pan. (You can ask your butcher to prepare them for you.)

Melt half the butter. Peel and chop the apples and onions and cook gently till soft. Add the stoned chopped prunes, breadcrumbs, rosemary and seasoning.

Spread the filling over two of the prepared tenderloins and cover with the remaining two. Tie firmly with fine string. Melt the rest of the butter in a roasting tin or large flameproof casserole and quickly brown the tenderloins in it. Pour over the wine and put the meat into a 350°F (180°C, Mark 4) oven for 1½ hours.

When the cooking is completed transfer the meat to a serving dish. Add the cream to the juices in the pan and blend well. This sauce can be poured over the meat or handed round separately.

Roast Pork with Baked Stuffed Apples

A LEG OR LOIN OF PORK	1 TSP SAGE
SALT	4 OZ (100 G) BREADCRUMBS
2 TBSP LARD OR DRIPPING	6 SMALL FIRM DESSERT
1 SMALL ONION	APPLES
1 OZ (25 G) BUTTER	

Score the rind of the pork and rub it all over with salt. Set the oven to 425°F (220°C, Mark 7) and when heated, put the lard or dripping in a roasting tin to melt. When it is smoking hot, lay the pork in the tin and baste well to seal. After 15 minutes, reduce the heat to 375°F (190°C, Mark 5) and roast for 35 minutes per pound, plus an extra 35 minutes.

Chop the onion finely and cook gently in the butter till soft but not brown. Stir in the sage and breadcrumbs. Core the apples and score round the centre of each one as this will prevent bursting. Stuff them with the sage and onion mixture. In the last 35 minutes set them round the joint, baste with the dripping and return to the oven until the cooking time is complete.

Carve the pork into slices and arrange on a serving dish surrounded by the apples. Make a thickened gravy from the juices and serve separately.

Pork and Oat Goulash

I MEDIUM ONION
2 OZ (50 G) DRIPPING
1½ LB (700 G) CUBED PORK
2 GREEN PEPPERS
2 DESSERT APPLES
I CLOVE OF GARLIC

½ PT (275 ML) LIGHT STOCK
½ PT (275 ML) WHITE WINE
I DESSERTSPOON TOMATO
   PURÉE
4 OZ (100 G) ROLLED OATS
SALT AND PEPPER

Peel and slice the onion. Melt the dripping in a flameproof casserole and brown the meat all over. Take it out and fry the onions till soft, then add the peppers, cut in thin strips, the peeled chopped apples and the crushed garlic. When they are all soft, add the browned meat and mix well. Pour in the stock, wine and tomato purée. Sprinkle the oats over the liquid, season to taste and cook at 300°F (150°C, Mark 2) for about 2 hours.

Serve with buttered noodles.

Danish Curried Pork

1½ LB (700 G) CUBED PORK
I ONION
I OZ (25 G) BUTTER
2 TSP CURRY POWDER
1½ OZ (40 G) FLOUR

4 DESSERT APPLES
8 OZ (225 G) BUTTON
   MUSHROOMS
¼ PT (150 ML) DOUBLE
   CREAM

Put the pork in a flameproof casserole or pan and cover with salted water. Bring to the boil and simmer for about an hour, or till tender. Chop the onion finely and cook gently in the butter till soft and transparent. Stir in the curry powder and cook for another minute, then stir in the flour and gradually add the pork stock, stirring constantly. Peel, core and chop the apples and add to the stock, along with the whole mushrooms. Simmer for 10 minutes and then add the pork, reheat and stir in the cream.

Serve with boiled rice.

Pork, Apple
and Raisin Casserole

BACON FAT FOR FRYING	2 OZ (50 G) RAISINS, SOAKED
4 BONELESS PORK CHOPS	IN WATER
8 PORK SAUSAGES	SALT AND PEPPER
1 LB (450 G) COOKING APPLES	¼ PT (150 ML) ORANGE JUICE
1 LB (450 G) ONIONS	

Melt the fat and brown the chops and sausages. Peel, core and slice the apples and peel and slice the onions. Take out the meat and add the onions, apples and raisins to the fat. Cook gently for about 5 minutes. Season to taste.

In a large casserole or baking dish put a third of the apple mixture, then the chops, another layer of mixture, the sausages and the remaining mixture. Pour over the orange juice and cover the dish. Bake at 325°F (170°C, Mark 3) for 1½ hours.

Serve with plain boiled potatoes or rice and a green vegetable to counteract the sweetness of the juices.

Pork Chops with
Cheese and Apple Stuffing

Stuffing

1 DESSERT APPLE	2 TBSP SEASONED FLOUR
1 OZ (25 G) CHEESE, GRATED	1 EGG, BEATEN
2 OZ (50 G) COOKED RICE	2 OZ (50 G) FINE
A PINCH EACH OF DRIED	BREADCRUMBS
SAGE, ROSEMARY AND	FAT FOR FRYING
BASIL	
SALT AND PEPPER	*To serve*
	SLICES OF TOMATO AND
4 PORK LOIN CHOPS	LEMON
COCKTAIL STICKS	SPRIGS OF PARSLEY

With a sharp knife cut through the sides of the chops to form a pocket. Peel and grate the apple, and mix with the cheese, rice, herbs and seasoning. Stuff the pockets with this mixture and close the openings with cocktail sticks. Dip each chop into the seasoned flour, then into the egg and finally into the breadcrumbs. Fry them in the hot fat, allowing 10–15 minutes each side.

Serve the chops decorated with slices of tomato and lemon and sprigs of parsley.

Pork Chops Charlevoix

This recipe is a speciality of Charlevoix County, Quebec.

8 THICK PORK CHOPS
SEASONED FLOUR
FAT FOR FRYING
3 TBSP MAPLE SYRUP
½ PT (275 ML) APPLE JUICE
2 DESSERT APPLES

Coat the chops in seasoned flour and brown in the fat. Pour in the maple syrup and apple juice. Cover and cook for ½ hour at 350°F (180°C, Mark 4). Quarter and core the apples and place a piece on each chop. Baste with the juices and cook, uncovered, for a further ½ hour. The apples should be soft.

Serve with boiled potatoes and a green vegetable.

Suffolk Medley Hotpot

2 PORK KIDNEYS	1 OZ (25 G) FAT
1 LARGE COOKING APPLE	½ TSP DRIED SAGE
1 LARGE ONION	SALT AND PEPPER
2 LARGE POTATOES	1 OZ (25 G) FLOUR
1½ LB (700 G) LEAN PORK, CUBED	½ PT (275 ML) DRY CIDER
	1 OZ (25 G) BUTTER

Chop the kidneys into four pieces. Peel and slice the apple, onion and potatoes. Brown the pork in the fat and transfer it to a large pie dish. Fry the kidneys and onion slices, adding more fat if necessary, and mix them with the pork, along with the apple slices, sage, salt and pepper. Stir the flour into the fat, blend thoroughly and gradually add the cider. Pour this sauce over the meat and top with the potato slices, arranged to overlap each other. Dot with butter and bake at 375°F (190°C, Mark 5) for about 1½ hours.

This dish is almost a meal in itself and needs only a green vegetable as an accompaniment.

> **I often wished that all my causes were apple-pie causes.**
> John Scott, Lord Eldon

Baked Onions
with Cheesy Pork Mince

6 MEDIUM ONIONS
FAT FOR FRYING
1 LB (450 G) MINCED PORK
1 TBSP FLOUR
2 TBSP TOMATO PURÉE
SALT AND PEPPER

½ PT (275 ML) STOCK OR
  CIDER
1 LARGE COOKING APPLE,
  GRATED
3 OZ (75 G) GRATED CHEESE

Peel the onions, taking care not to sever the root. Put them in a pan of cold water and bring to the boil; reduce the heat, cover and simmer for 30 minutes.

Meanwhile, melt the fat in a frying-pan and brown the pork for a few minutes, working it well with a wooden spoon to break it up. Add the flour and tomato purée, season well and cook for another minute; then pour in the stock or cider. Finally add the grated apple and cheese.

Drain the onions and arrange them in a large shallow oven dish. Pour the mince mixture over them and bake at 350°F (180°C, Mark 4) for 1 hour.

Serve with mashed potatoes or boiled rice.

Bacon Chops
with Glazed Apple Rings

4 OZ (100 G) SUGAR

4 TBSP CIDER

1 LARGE FIRM APPLE

4 BACON CHOPS

OIL

First prepare the caramel by warming the sugar in a heavy frying-pan over a low heat till it melts and caramelizes. Add the cider carefully and stir until you have a rich brown syrup. Peel and core the apple and slice into eight rings. Cook them in the syrup over a low heat for 3–4 minutes, turning once.

Meanwhile brush the bacon chops with oil and grill for about 8 minutes, turning once. Garnish each chop with 2 apple rings and serve with a green salad.

Curried Lamb

This is a useful recipe for using up the remains of a joint. It is also very quick and simple to prepare.

3 RASHERS BACON

2 SMALL DESSERT APPLES

2 STICKS CELERY

1 MEDIUM ONION

2 TBSP FLOUR

1 TBSP CURRY POWDER

½ TSP SALT

½ TSP TURMERIC

¼ PT (150 ML) CHICKEN
  STOCK

½ PT (275 ML) MILK

1 LB (450 G) COLD COOKED
  LAMB

2 TSP SUGAR

1 TBSP LEMON JUICE

8 OZ (225 G) RICE COOKED IN
  1 PT (575 ML) SALTED
  WATER

Chop the bacon and fry in a large pan. Peel, core and chop the apples.

Chop the celery and onion and add, with the apples, to the bacon. Stir over a low heat, adding a little fat if necessary, until the onions are soft. Stir in the flour, curry powder, salt and turmeric, and when absorbed gradually add the stock and milk. Stir constantly until the sauce thickens. Cut the lamb into cubes and add to the sauce with the sugar and lemon juice. Cover and simmer for 10 minutes. Serve with boiled rice.

Fried Liver
with Apples and Onions

This dish is a speciality of Berlin. It is very quick and economical as everything can be cooked together in the same pan.

2 ONIONS
FAT FOR FRYING
I LB (450 G) LAMB'S LIVER
SEASONED FLOUR
I DESSERT APPLE

Peel the onions and slice them into rings. Melt the fat in a frying-pan. Fry the onions in the fat till soft, and then push them to the side of the pan. Coat the pieces of liver in the seasoned flour and fry them till brown and crisp on each side. Core and slice the apple and fry for a few minutes till golden. Serve immediately.

Fried potatoes make a good accompaniment to this dish.

Stuffed Liver

8 LARGE SLICES LAMB'S LIVER	PINCH OF DRIED MARJORAM
4 OZ (100 G) STREAKY BACON	½ PT (275 ML) STOCK
I CARROT	2 TBSP NATURAL BRAN
I ONION	SALT AND PEPPER
I DESSERT APPLE	FAT FOR FRYING

Wash the liver, pat dry and, using a very sharp knife, cut a pocket in each slice. Chop the bacon very finely and fry in its own fat. Peel the carrot and onion and core the apple. Chop them very finely, sprinkle with marjoram and add to the bacon. Cook till soft and then pour in the stock. Simmer for 15 minutes and stir in the bran. Season with salt and pepper. Stuff the liver slices with some of this mixture and fry in a separate pan for about 5 minutes each side. Serve the stuffed liver arranged on a bed of the remaining vegetables.

Sausage and Apple Pie

In this old recipe the sausage meat doubles as meat content and pastry.

8 OZ (225 G) COOKING APPLES	1 OZ (25 G) BUTTER
1 ONION OR LEEK	SALT AND PEPPER
1 TOMATO	3 TBSP CHUTNEY
8 OZ (225 G) POTATOES	1 LB (450 G) SAUSAGE MEAT

Peel, core and chop the apples and vegetables. Fry gently in the butter for 5–10 minutes or until soft but not brown. Spoon them over the base of a shallow, greased, ovenproof dish and season. Spread the chutney over the vegetables.

Roll out the sausage meat on a floured board to about ½ in (1 cm) thickness, to fit over the dish. Lay it over the vegetables and bake at 400°F (200°C, Mark 6) for 45 minutes.

Cod Fillets
with Apple Stuffing

4 COD FILLETS, ABOUT 6 OZ	JUICE OF ½ LEMON
(175 G) EACH	SALT AND PEPPER
1 LARGE APPLE	1 TBSP CHOPPED PARSLEY
4 OZ (100 G) BREADCRUMBS	1 EGG

| ½ PT (275 ML) MILK | I OZ (25 G) FLOUR |
| I OZ (25 G) BUTTER | I OZ (25 G) GRATED CHEESE |

Set the oven to 375°F (190°C, Mark 5). Skin the fish, wash it and pat dry with kitchen paper. Grate the apple and mix with 3 oz (75 g) of the breadcrumbs, and the lemon juice, seasoning and parsley. Beat the egg and stir into the mixture. Spread a quarter of the mixture on each fillet and roll it up. Lay in a shallow buttered ovenproof dish, pour in half the milk and bake for 20 minutes.

Remove from the oven; pour off the liquid and reserve it. Melt the butter in a pan, blend in the flour and gradually add the fish liquor and the remaining milk, stirring all the time till the sauce thickens. Pour the sauce over the fish. Mix the cheese with the remaining breadcrumbs, sprinkle over the dish and put it under the grill until golden brown. Serve at once.

Quick Fish Curry

I LB (450 G) WHITE FISH	I DESSERT APPLE
FILLETS	I OZ (25 G) BUTTER
JUICE OF ½ LEMON	2 TSP CURRY POWDER
SALT	3 TBSP EVAPORATED MILK
2 MEDIUM ONIONS	

Wash the fish and pat dry with kitchen paper. Sprinkle them with lemon juice and salt. Chop the onions and apple and cook gently in the butter for about 5 minutes. Then stir in the curry powder and evaporated milk. Spread some of this mixture over the base of a shallow baking dish, lay the fish on top and cover with the remaining curry mixture. Bake at 350°F (180°C, Mark 4) for 15 minutes.

Serve with boiled rice.

Apple
and Cheese Charlotte

This is from my grandmother's old recipe book and makes a very filling substitute for a meat dish.

8 OZ (225 G) COOKING APPLES	SALT AND PEPPER
I SMALL ONION	4 OZ (100 G) BREADCRUMBS
I OZ (25 G) BUTTER	3 OZ (75 G) GRATED CHEESE
3 OZ (75 G) LENTILS	

Set the oven to 400°F (200°C, Mark 6). Peel, core and slice the apples and chop the onion finely. Melt the butter and cook the apples and onion in it till soft; then add the lentils and ½ pt (275 ml) water. Cook until the water is absorbed – this takes 10–15 minutes. Season well and beat till smooth and creamy. Mix the crumbs and the cheese together and season. Fill a buttered pie dish with alternate layers, finishing with the cheese mixture. Bake for 10 minutes.

9
Pastry Dishes

But I, when I undress me
Each night upon my knees,
Will ask the Lord to bless me
With apple pie and cheese.

EUGENE FIELD

here are so many recipes for apple pies, tarts, flans and dumplings, that a whole book, rather than a mere chapter, could be dedicated to the subject of apples with pastry.

Even the well-known apple pie, more quoted in literature than any other apple dish, varies throughout England in its form and accompaniments. For example, in 1697, Celia Fiennes records in her diary, *Through England on a Side Saddle* (published 1888), that in Cornwall she ate

West Country Tarts: its an apple pye with a Custard all on the top, its ye most acceptable entertainment it Could be made me. They scald their Creame and milk in most parts of those Countrys, and so its a sort of Clouted Creame as we call it, with a little sugar and soe put on ye top of ye apple Pye.

The oldest English recipe for an apple tart is found in the fourteenth-century *The Form of Cury* and is entitled, 'For to make tartys in applis'. The recipe is simple:

Take gode Applys and gode Spycis and Figys and reysons and Perys [pears] and wan they are wel ybrayed coulourd with Safron wel and do yt in a cofyn [pastry case] and do yt forth to bake well.

The dried fruit was used to bulk out the tart filling. No quantities are specified here.

Robert May in *The Accomplish'd Cook* (1665) gives recipes for very large pies and tarts using thirty or forty apples. These were designed for banquets at a time when food was plentiful, appetites large, and fibre and cholesterol unknown.

Many of the traditional English savoury apple pies (e.g. Shropshire fidget, Devonshire squab or Cheshire pork pies) were served to harvesters and so had to be both large and filling. This time the apples were the 'bulking-out' ingredient, often stretching a meagre meat content. For this reason there are no correct versions and the quantities of meat and apples can be adjusted to suit taste and outlay.

Two unusual Scottish pies are worthy of mention. Elizabeth Cleland's 'Christmas Apple Pie with Chestnuts and Almonds' from *A New and Easy Method of Cooking* (1759) and Susannah McIver's

'Apple Pie with Potatoes', from *Cookery and Pastry* (1786) are both flavoured with candied orange, lemon peel and sugar. They are reminiscent of the medieval recipe in their bizarre sweet and savoury mixtures and the bulking-out technique.

Berries, such as blackberries or whortleberries, also serve this purpose, and each combination provides another facet to the rich variety of traditional British apple pies.

Abroad, the choice is equally bewildering, especially in apple-growing areas such as Normandy. European recipes were taken by emigrants to their adopted countries, where they were modified and became new traditional recipes.

Pastry

Recipes for four types of pastry used in this chapter are given here to avoid repetition. The quantities of pastry given in the ingredient lists refer to the weight of the flour content, not to the weight of the prepared dough. Frozen pastry, on the other hand, is measured by its total weight, so you should buy more of it to allow for the difference. With shortcrust pastry, about half as much again is needed; with flaky pastry and pâte brisée twice the amount.

Shortcrust Pastry

6 OZ (175 G) PLAIN FLOUR
PINCH OF SALT
3 OZ (75 G) BUTTER, MARGARINE OR FAT,
OR A MIXTURE OF THESE

Sift the flour and salt into a bowl. Cut the butter or fat into small pieces. With your fingertips rub these into the flour until the mixture resembles breadcrumbs. Make a well in the centre and add about 2 tbsp water, mixing it quickly into the flour with a knife or metal spoon. Add more water if necessary and mix to a dough, which should be firm and smooth but not sticky. Turn on to a floured surface or board and knead the pastry till smooth. Wrap it in clingfilm or foil and chill for 30 minutes before using.

For 8 oz (225 g) measure, use the following quantities:

8 OZ (225 G) FLOUR
PINCH OF SALT
4 OZ (100 G) BUTTER OR FAT
3 TBSP COLD WATER

Apples are sweet when they are plucked in the Gardiner's absence.
Eve liked no apple in the Garden so well as the forbidden.
T. Adams, *Devil's Banquet* (1614)

Pâte Brisée

(FRENCH FLAN PASTRY)

6 OZ (175 G) PLAIN FLOUR
PINCH OF SALT
2–3 EGG YOLKS
3 TBSP CASTER SUGAR
4 OZ (100 G) BUTTER

Sift the flour and salt on to a working surface or board. Make a well in the centre and add the rest of the ingredients. Using your fingertips, work these into the flour as quickly as possible, drawing in the flour from the sides until it is all absorbed. Knead very gently till it is smooth and then chill. This pastry breaks easily, so handle it as little as possible.

Suet Pastry

This pastry should be used immediately, so do not make it in advance.

8 OZ (225 G) SELF-RAISING FLOUR
PINCH OF SALT
4 OZ (100 G) SHREDDED SUET

Sift the flour and salt into a bowl. Add the suet and mix it in. Make a well in the centre and gradually add ¼ pt (150 ml) water, mixing it quickly into the flour until the dough leaves the sides clean. Turn it on to a floured surface or board and knead lightly till smooth.

Flaky Pastry

8 OZ (225 G) FLOUR
PINCH OF SALT

6 OZ (175 G) BUTTER, MARGARINE OR LARD, OR A MIXTURE OF
THESE

Sift the flour and salt into a bowl. Cut up the fats into four equal portions. Rub one portion into the flour, as for shortcrust. Make a well in the centre and add about ¼ pt (150 ml) water, mix quickly with a knife to a firm dough, and add more water if needed. Turn the dough on to a floured surface or board and knead till smooth.

Roll out the dough to an oblong shape three times as long as it is wide. Take a second portion of the fat, cut it in small pieces and arrange these evenly over two thirds of the dough, but leave clear a margin of ½ in (1 cm) at the edges. Fold the uncovered third over to the middle and fold the other end over this one. Press down the open edges with a rolling-pin; roll it out again to a strip the size of the original. Repeat the process with a third portion of fat and wrap the pastry in clingfilm or polythene. Leave it to rest for 15–20 minutes in a cool place.

Repeat the process with the remaining fat. Let the pastry rest for at least ½ hour before using.

Baking Blind

When a recipe calls for a cooked pastry case, the pastry should first be baked blind.

Line the pastry into the prepared flan tin and prick it. Cover the base with greaseproof paper and fill it with dried beans or rice. Alternatively, fill the pastry case with crumpled foil. Bake the pastry at 400°F (200°C, Mark 6) for 15 minutes, lift out the greaseproof paper or foil and replace the pastry in the oven for a further 5 minutes to dry out the base.

Lamb and Apple Plate Pie

This pie is a good way of using up the remains of a Sunday roast. Leftover pork can also be used, but in this case substitute dried sage for the rosemary.

8 OZ (225 G) SHORTCRUST PASTRY (p. 108)	I TBSP SUGAR
	I TSP TOMATO PURÉE
8 OZ (225 G) LEFTOVER COOKED LAMB	½ TSP DRIED ROSEMARY
	SALT AND PEPPER
8 OZ (225 G) COOKING APPLES	2–3 TBSP STOCK
I ONION	A LITTLE MILK
I TBSP RAISINS	

Roll out half the pastry and use to line a large buttered pie plate. Mince together the lamb, apple and onion, and add the raisins, sugar, tomato purée, rosemary, seasoning and stock. Mix well and spoon it into the pastry case. Roll out the remaining pastry and cover the pie. Press the edges together, trim and flute them and cut steam vents. Brush with milk and bake at 400°F (200°C, Mark 6) for 30 minutes.

Devonshire Squab Pie

An inexplicable name, since a squab is a young pigeon and this recipe is always made with lamb!

6 LAMB CHUMP CHOPS	I TSP DRIED ROSEMARY
FAT FOR FRYING	I TBSP SUGAR
I LB (450 G) ONIONS	¼ PT (150 ML) STOCK
I LB (450 G) COOKING APPLES	8 OZ (225 G) SHORTCRUST PASTRY (p. 108)
SALT AND PEPPER	

Brown the chops quickly in the fat. Peel and slice the onions and apples. Lay three chops in a 2 pt (1 l) pie dish, season well and cover with half the onions, apples and rosemary. Repeat these layers, and sprinkle the top layer of apples with sugar. Pour in the stock, cover with the pastry (see Cheshire Pork Pie, below), and bake at 400°F (200°C, Mark 6) for 20 minutes and then reduce the heat to 350°F (180°C, Mark 4) for the next hour.

Cheshire Pork Pie

A version of this appears in John Farley's *The London Art of Cookery* (1783).

2 LB (1 KG) PIE PORK	I TSP DRIED SAGE
SEASONED FLOUR (WITH NUTMEG)	¼ PT (150 ML) WHITE WINE
FAT FOR FRYING	8 OZ (225 G) SHORTCRUST PASTRY (p. 108)
2 ONIONS	A LITTLE MILK OR BEATEN EGG
4 DESSERT APPLES	

Dice the pork, coat in seasoned flour and fry in the fat till sealed and golden brown. Peel and chop the onions and apples. Fill a 2 pt (1 l) pie dish with alternating layers of pork, onions, apples and sage, and pour in the wine. Roll out the pastry. Dampen the rim of the pie dish, cut strips from the edge of the pastry and press these on to the rim. Brush with water and cover the pie with pastry. Trim and flute the edges, using any excess pastry to make decorative leaves, cut steam vents in the centre of the pie and brush it with milk or beaten egg. Bake at 400°F (200°C, Mark 6) for 20 minutes, then reduce the heat to 375°F (190°C, Mark 5) and bake for 1 hour. If the pastry becomes too brown, cover it with kitchen foil.

Shropshire Fidget Pie

The meaning of 'fidget' is unknown. This is a Shropshire speciality, traditionally served at harvest time. The amount of meat varied and when times were hard, it was left out altogether. At prosperous times, however, it was supplemented by lamb chops.

2 LB (1 KG) SLIPPER OF
  GAMMON OR BACON JOINT
1 LB (450 G) POTATOES
8 OZ (225 G) ONIONS
8 OZ (225 G) COOKING APPLES
1 TBSP BROWN SUGAR

FRESHLY GROUND BLACK
  PEPPER
¼ PT (150 ML) CIDER
8 OZ (225 G) SHORTCRUST
  PASTRY (p. 108)
1 EGG, BEATEN

Put the gammon or bacon into a pan of cold water, bring to the boil and drain. De-rind the joint and dice the meat. Peel and slice the potatoes, onions and apples. In a 2 pt (1 l) pie dish, layer the meat, onions, apples and potatoes until all ingredients are used up. Sprinkle with sugar and pepper, pour on the cider and cover with the pastry lid. (See Cheshire Pork Pie, p. 113.) Cut slits in the pastry and brush with beaten egg. Bake at 400°F (200°C, Mark 6) for 20 minutes, then lower the heat to 350°F (180°C, Mark 4) and bake for another hour.

Like the sweet apple which reddens upon the topmost bough
A-top the topmost twig – which the pluckers forgot, somehow –
Forgot it not, nay, but got it not, for none could get it now.
D. G. Rossetti, 'Beauty, a Combination from Sappho'

East Riding Pudding
with Spicy Apple Sauce

8 OZ (225 G) SUET PASTRY
  (p. 110)
1½ LB (700 G) BELLY OF PORK
1 LARGE ONION
1 LB (450 G) POTATOES
SALT AND PEPPER
DRIED SAGE

Sauce

1 SMALL ONION
1 OZ (25 G) BUTTER
1 SMALL COOKING APPLE
SALT AND PEPPER
1 DESSERTSPOON SUGAR
1 TSP WORCESTERSHIRE
  SAUCE

First make the pastry and use three quarters of it to line a 2 pt (1 l) greased pudding basin. Cut the pork into cubes, peel and chop the onion, peel and finely slice the potatoes. Fill the basin with layers of pork, onion, seasoning, sage and potatoes. Repeat the layers, pour in 2 tbsp water and cover with the rest of the pastry. Cover the dish with a cloth or with foil, allowing space for the pastry to rise. Tie it securely with string and steam for at least 3 hours.

To make the sauce, peel and finely chop the onion and cook it gently in the butter. Peel, core and slice the apple, add to the onion and cook for a few minutes till soft. Beat with a wooden spoon, add the seasoning, sugar and Worcestershire sauce, and serve hot with the pudding.

Taffety Tart

One of the oldest recipes, this is adapted from *The Queen's Closet Opened* (1656).

8 OZ (225 G) FLAKY PASTRY
  (p. 110)
3–4 DESSERT APPLES
2 TBSP SUGAR
GRATED RIND OF 1 LEMON

Topping

2 OZ (50 G) BUTTER
2 OZ (50 G) SUGAR
1 TSP ROSEWATER

Set the oven to 400°F (200°C, Mark 6). Divide the pastry into three equal portions. Roll out one of these to a rectangle about 7 × 11 in (18 × 28 cm) and lift it carefully on to a wetted baking sheet. Peel, core and slice the apples. Lay half of them on the pastry and sprinkle with half of the sugar and lemon rind. Roll out another layer of pastry to fit on top and repeat the process, topping the tart with the last pastry layer. Bake for 20 minutes. Meanwhile, prepare the topping: cream the butter and sugar together till fluffy and then beat in the rosewater. Take the tart from the oven and, if it has risen unevenly, press it down gently. Spread with the topping and return to the oven for a further 10 minutes.

Serve warm or cold with cream.

Elizabethan pie-crust patterns

What's this? a sleeve? 'tis like a demi-cannon.
What! up and down, carv'd like an apple tart?
Here's snip and nip, and cut and slish and slash
Like to a censer in a barber's shop.

Shakespeare, *The Taming of the Shrew*

Old English Pippin Pie

SHORTCRUST PASTRY (p. 108)
MADE WITH 10 OZ (275 G)
FLOUR
2 LB (1 KG) FIRM DESSERT
APPLES
3 TBSP CASTER SUGAR
GRATED RIND OF 1 LEMON
1 TSP CINNAMON
6 CLOVES

1 TBSP ORANGE JUICE
1 TBSP CIDER

Glaze

2 OZ (50 G) SUGAR
2 OZ (50 G) BUTTER
1 TSP ROSEWATER OR
ORANGE-FLOWER WATER

Prepare the shortcrust pastry and, when rested, divide it in half. Roll out one portion and line a large, greased pie plate with it. Peel, core and slice the apples, and arrange a layer on the pastry. Sprinkle with some sugar, lemon rind, cinnamon and cloves and moisten with the mixed juice and cider. Repeat this process until the ingredients are used up, then roll out the second batch of pastry and cover the pie. Seal the edges and flute them. Cut steam vents and put the unglazed pie in a 375°F (190°C, Mark 5) oven for 45 minutes. Remove the pie when cooked and brush with the glaze (see Taffety Tart, p. 115). Return the pie to the oven for a further 10 minutes.

Serve warm with cream or clotted cream.

Old English Pippin Tart

6 OZ (175 G) SHORTCRUST PASTRY (p. 108)
½ PT (275 ML) WHITE WINE
4 TBSP CASTER SUGAR
½ STICK CINNAMON
3 CLOVES
6 DESSERT APPLES
4 PIECES CRYSTALLIZED GINGER
4 TBSP APPLE JELLY

Make the pastry, line an 8 in (20 cm) flan ring with it and bake blind. Make a syrup with the wine, sugar, cinnamon and cloves. Peel and core the apples and slice them into the syrup. Slice the ginger pieces and add to the pan. Cover and cook very gently for about 10 minutes or until the apples are soft. Warm the jelly with a little of the wine syrup. Brush some over the inside of the flan case, drain the apple and ginger slices and spoon them into the case. Glaze with the remaining jelly.

Serve cold with cream.

Eighteenth-century Apple Flan

The spongy filling for this flan is also very good served on its own.

6 OZ (175 G) SHORTCRUST
   PASTRY (p. 108)
I LB (450 G) APPLE PURÉE
   (p. 43)
5 EGGS
4 OZ (100 G) BUTTER,
   SOFTENED

2 TSP ORANGE-FLOWER
   WATER
2–3 TBSP SUGAR
GRATED RIND OF AN ORANGE

Line an 8 in (20 cm) flan ring with the pastry and bake blind at 400°F (200°C, Mark 6) for 20 minutes. Meanwhile, prepare the filling. Beat the eggs thoroughly and combine with the apple purée. Add the butter, cut into small pieces, and the remaining ingredients. Blend well and pour into the prepared pastry case. Bake for a further ½ hour.

Serve warm with cream.

Apple Amber

6 OZ (175 G) SHORTCRUST
   PASTRY (p. 108)
I LB (450 G) COOKING APPLES
GRATED RIND AND JUICE OF
   ½ LEMON

I OZ (25 G) BUTTER
4 OZ (100 G) GRANULATED
   SUGAR
2 EGGS
4 OZ (100 G) CASTER SUGAR

Line an 8 in (20 cm) flan tin with the pastry and bake blind. Meanwhile, peel, core and slice the apples and cook to a purée with the lemon rind and juice. Beat in the butter and granulated sugar, cool slightly and beat in the egg yolks. Pour this mixture into the pastry case. Whip the egg whites till stiff, beat in a little caster sugar and then fold in the rest. Spread this meringue on top of the filling and bake at 300°F (150°C, Mark 2) for 35–40 minutes.

Serve hot or cold with cream, yoghurt or ice-cream.

And al was for an appil
An appil that he tok.
Anon (fifteenth century)

Dumplings,
Turnovers and Squares

Apple dumplings have always been a popular, filling dessert for cold weather. Like baked apples, they seem traditionally English, but are equally popular in France under the name of *bourdelots*, and in Germany, where they are intriguingly called 'apples in dressing-gowns'. Shortcrust pastry is usually used, although puff or suet pastry is also possible, and the apples may be cookers or a large dessert variety. The peeled, cored apple is simply set on a square of pastry, with a filling of sugar, jam or butter if desired; the pastry is then wrapped round the apple and the ends tucked into the core hole. Reverse the apple so that the joins are underneath, brush with milk and bake at 400°F (200°C, Mark 6) for about 40 minutes.

For turnovers (French *chaussons*, German *Apfeltaschen*, or apple pockets) a circle or oval of pastry is used and the apples are chopped or grated and mixed with sugar, cinnamon and perhaps a handful of raisins. Moisten the edges of the pastry, seal and brush with egg yolk. Bake as for apple dumplings.

Another popular shape is the square, *carré aux pommes*. A similar recipe, *gâche aux pommes*, is a speciality of Guernsey. The pastry is divided in half, rolled out to a square and covered with apple slices sprinkled with sugar and cinnamon. The edges are moistened and the second square of pastry fitted on top. Again, brush with egg yolk and bake as for dumplings.

All these should be served warm with cream.

Tarte aux Pommes

6 OZ (175 G) SHORTCRUST PASTRY (p. 108),
USING BEER INSTEAD OF WATER
4 DESSERT APPLES
2 OZ (50 G) BUTTER
3 OZ (75 G) SOFT BROWN SUGAR
I EGG

Line an 8 in (20 cm) flan ring with the pastry. Peel, core and thinly slice the apples. Arrange them in concentric circles on the pastry. Beat together the remaining ingredients and spread over the apples. Bake at 400°F (200°C, Mark 6) for 35 minutes.

Serve warm or cold with cream, yoghurt or *crème fraîche*.

Tarte Normande

6 OZ (175 G) PÂTE BRISÉE	½ PT (275 ML) MILK
(p. 110)	A LITTLE VANILLA ESSENCE
2 EGGS	3 DESSERT APPLES
2½ OZ (60 G) CASTER SUGAR	3 OZ (75 G) SUGAR
1½ OZ (40 G) CORNFLOUR	1 OZ (25 G) BUTTER

Chill the pastry. Beat together the eggs, caster sugar and cornflour. Meanwhile bring to the boil the milk and vanilla essence, pour it on to the egg mixture, blend thoroughly and return to the pan, stirring till the mixture thickens. Let it cool.

Line an 8 in (20 cm) flan ring with the pastry, spread with the cooled custard and finish with circles of thinly sliced apples. Sprinkle with sugar, dot with butter and bake at 400°F (200°C, Mark 6) for 25–30 minutes.

If preferred a thick apple purée can be used to fill the tart instead of the custard.

Serve hot or cold with cream, yoghurt or *crème fraîche*.

Tarte des Demoiselles Tatin

This classic recipe proves that necessity is indeed the mother of invention. The Tatin sisters owned a hotel in the village of Lamotte Beuvron in the Solonge area. Their cooking facilities were limited to an open fire and a range, which made the conventional preparation of an apple tart impossible. However, by inverting the tart and covering the hotplate with a metal dome, they surmounted this difficulty and

gave us this delicious recipe. Tarte Tatin must be cooked in a metal tin as the conduction of heat is very important. But it must not be a loose-bottomed tin, otherwise the juices will run out!

3 OZ (75 G) BUTTER
3 OZ (75 G) ICING SUGAR
2 LB (1 KG) DESSERT APPLES
1 TSP CINNAMON
6 OZ (175 G) PÂTE BRISÉE (p. 110)
1 EGG YOLK, BEATEN

Use a 9–10 in (23–25 cm) round tin, *not* loose bottomed; butter the tin liberally and sprinkle with 1 oz (25 g) icing sugar. Peel, core and slice the apples. Put half in the tin, dot with more butter and sprinkle with sugar and cinnamon. Use up the remaining ingredients to make another layer. Cover with the pastry and brush it with the beaten egg yolk. Bake at 400°F (200°C, Mark 6) for 10 minutes, then reduce the heat to 375°F (190°C, Mark 5) and bake for a further 35 minutes. Watch it carefully, and cover the pastry with foil if it browns too quickly.

Remove the tart from the oven, place the serving dish over it and invert quickly. The apples should be soft and caramelized.

Serve at once with cream, yoghurt or *crème fraîche*.

Alsace Apple Flan

6 OZ (175 G) SHORTCRUST PASTRY (p. 108), BUT USE WHITE WINE INSTEAD OF WATER
4 DESSERT APPLES
1 TBSP SUGAR
1 EGG
1 OZ (25 G) ICING SUGAR
1 OZ (25 G) CASTER SUGAR
GRATED RIND OF 1 LEMON
A FEW DROPS OF VANILLA ESSENCE
¼ PT (150 ML) SOURED CREAM

Use the pastry to line an 8 in (20 cm) deep flan ring or spring-clip pan. Peel, halve and core the apples and score the rounded sides at intervals of ¼ in (½ cm). Arrange them on the pastry, scored sides uppermost. Sprinkle with 1 tbsp sugar, and bake at 400°F (200°C, Mark 6) for 30 minutes.

Beat together the egg, icing sugar, caster sugar, lemon rind and vanilla till foamy, and then fold in the soured cream; pour into the pastry case and bake for a further 10 minutes.

Serve warm or cold with cream.

Zürich Parsonage Flan

This is a very large flan, serving 12 people.

8 OZ (225 G) SHORTCRUST PASTRY (P. 108)	½ TSP BAKING POWDER
3 EGGS	2 OZ (50 G) FRESHLY GROUND ALMONDS
6 OZ (175 G) CASTER SUGAR	1 LB (450 G) SMALL DESSERT APPLES
1 TBSP LEMON JUICE	
1 TBSP RUM	1 OZ (25 G) MELTED BUTTER
1 LARGE COOKING APPLE	ICING SUGAR
1 OZ (25 G) FLOUR	

Roll out the pastry and use to line a 9 × 13 in (23 × 33 cm) swiss-roll tin. Bake blind at 450°F (220°C, Mark 7) for 15 minutes. Separate the eggs and beat the yolks with the caster sugar for about 10 minutes till thick and light in colour. Add the lemon juice and rum. Peel the cooking apple and grate coarsely over the mixture. Whip the egg whites to a snow and fold into the mixture with the apple. Sift together the flour and baking powder and sprinkle over the mixture along with the ground almonds. Fold everything in gently and pour the mixture into the pastry case. Peel, halve and core the dessert apples and score the rounded sides at ¼ in (½ cm) intervals. Arrange them in the almond mixture, scored side uppermost, and brush the tops with melted butter. Bake at 350°F (180°C, Mark 4) for 35 minutes. On removing from the oven, sprinkle the flan at once with sifted icing sugar.

Serve warm or cold with cream.

Apple Strudel

The first filling is that of a conventional apple strudel. The second is rather different; the soured cream and lemon juice give it a sharp, refreshing flavour.

Pastry

8 OZ (225 G) PLAIN FLOUR
PINCH OF SALT
1 EGG, BEATEN
1 TBSP OIL
2 OZ (50 G) MELTED BUTTER

For the pastry, sift the flour and salt into a warm bowl. Make a well in the centre. Mix together the egg, oil and 4 tbsp warm water, pour into the well and quickly mix to soft but firm dough, adding more flour if it becomes sticky. Turn on to a floured surface and knead for about 10 minutes till smooth and elastic, then return it to the bowl. Cover with clingfilm and leave for about 30 minutes.

Lay out a clean tea-towel and dust it with flour. Put the dough in the centre and roll it out as thinly as possible; then, flouring the backs of your hands and slipping them under the pastry, carefully pull and stretch it from the centre outwards till you have a long paper-thin rectangle. If it tears, press the edges together again. Brush the surface with half the melted butter.

Filling 1	*Filling 2*
1 LB (450 G) APPLES	1 LB (450 G) APPLES
2 OZ (50 G) SUGAR	2 OZ (50 G) SUGAR
PINCH OF CINNAMON	PINCH OF CINNAMON
2 OZ (50 G) BREADCRUMBS	2 OZ (50 G) GROUND
2 OZ (50 G) RAISINS	ALMONDS
1 TBSP ORANGE JUICE	$\frac{1}{4}$ PT (150 ML) SOURED
GRATED RIND OF $\frac{1}{2}$ LEMON	CREAM
	GRATED RIND AND JUICE OF
	$\frac{1}{2}$ LEMON

For either filling, grate the apples and mix with the other ingredients. Spoon the chosen filling along the near edge of the pastry and then, lifting the tea-towel away from you, roll up the strudel like a swiss roll. Press down and trim the ends, then roll it on to a greased baking sheet, curling it to fit if necessary. Brush with the remaining melted butter and bake at 400°F (200°C, Mark 6) for 20 minutes, then reduce the heat to 375°F (190°C, Mark 5) and bake for a further 10 minutes.

Either version can be served warm or cold, with cream, yoghurt or *crème fraîche*.

Apple Pandowdy

An American apple pie flavoured with molasses or black treacle. The name derives from the process of 'dowdying' or breaking up the crust after cooking.

2 OZ (50 G) SUGAR	3 OZ (75 G) BLACK TREACLE
PINCH OF CINNAMON	2 TBSP WATER
PINCH OF NUTMEG	2 OZ (50 G) BUTTER
PINCH OF SALT	8 OZ (225 G) FLAKY PASTRY
1½ LB (700 G) COOKING	(p. 110)
APPLES	

Set the oven to 400°F (200°C, Mark 6). Mix together the sugar, spices and salt. Butter a 2 pt (1 l) pie or baking dish and peel, core and slice the apples into it, layering them with the sugar mixture. Now warm the remaining ingredients together and pour over the apples. Roll out the pastry and use to cover the pie dish (as for Cheshire Pork Pie, p. 113). Bake for 40 minutes, reducing the heat to 325°F (170°C, Mark 3) after 10 minutes. Remove the pie from the oven and make several deep cuts through the crust and filling. Return to the oven for a further 10 minutes. Just before serving, stir the crust into the apple filling.

Serve hot with cream or ice-cream.

Cassia lignea. 1. Blüthe. 2 Frucht. 3. 4. die Frucht alleine. 5 Kern. 6. Zimmet. Mutter-Zimmet.

Okanagan Apple and Lemon Flan

6 OZ (175 G) SHORTCRUST PASTRY (p. 108)	3 OZ (75 G) BROWN SUGAR
I LEMON	I TBSP FLOUR
3 DESSERT APPLES	PINCH OF SALT
I OZ (25 G) BUTTER	I EGG

Line an 8 in (20 cm) flan ring with the pastry and bake blind at 400°F (200°C, Mark 6) for 20 minutes. For the filling, grate the lemon rind and the peeled apples. Melt the butter in a pan over a gentle heat and stir in the sugar, flour, salt, grated apples, lemon rind and juice and the egg yolk. Whisk the egg white till stiff and fold in. Pour the filling into the flan case and bake at 350°F (180°C, Mark 4) for 25 minutes, or until firm.

Serve warm with cream.

Crumble-topped Apple Flan

6 OZ (175 G) SHORTCRUST PASTRY (p. 108)	I EGG
2 TBSP FLOUR	¼ PT (150 ML) SOURED CREAM
PINCH OF SALT	I TSP VANILLA ESSENCE
3 OZ (75 G) SUGAR	PINCH OF NUTMEG
	I LARGE COOKING APPLE

Topping
2 OZ (50 G) BUTTER
1½ OZ (40 G) FLOUR
3 OZ (75 G) SUGAR
I TSP CINNAMON

Line an 8 in (20 cm) flan ring with the pastry. Sift the flour, salt and sugar and beat in the egg, soured cream, vanilla essence and nutmeg.

Peel, core and dice the apple and stir into the mixture. Bake at 400°F (200°C, Mark 6) for 15 minutes and then reduce the heat to 350°F (180°C, Mark 4) for 30 minutes.

Meanwhile, prepare the topping. Rub the butter into the flour until the mixture resembles fine breadcrumbs. Mix in the sugar and cinnamon, sprinkle over the flan and return to the oven at 400°F for 10 minutes.

Serve warm with cream or ice-cream.

Winter Pie

This pie with its unusual combination of ingredients is a regional speciality of Nova Scotia, dating from the time when the early settlers had to utilize all available foods.

SHORTCRUST PASTRY (p. 108) MADE WITH 10 OZ (275 G) FLOUR	4 OZ (100 G) RAISINS
	3 TBSP VINEGAR
	1 OZ (25 G) BUTTER
1 TBSP CORNFLOUR	8 OZ (225 G) APPLE, GRATED
PINCH OF NUTMEG	2 OZ (50 G) CARROT, GRATED
PINCH OF CINNAMON	4 OZ (100 G) POTATO,
PINCH OF SALT	GRATED
4 OZ (100 G) BROWN SUGAR	

Grease a 9 in (23 cm) pie plate. Put the cornflour, spices, salt, sugar and raisins in a pan. Add the vinegar and 3 tbsp hot water, stir till blended, bring to the boil and cook gently for 5 minutes. Stir in the butter, and then the grated apple, carrot and potato. Leave to cool. Roll out half the pastry and line the pie plate with it. Spoon in the cooled filling, cover the pie with the remaining pastry and cut steam vents. Bake at 450°F (230°C, Mark 8) for 10 minutes and then reduce the heat to 350°F (180°C, Mark 4) for 40 minutes.

Serve warm with cream or yoghurt.

From the egg to the apples.
Ab ovo usque ad mala (from the first to the last dish)
Horace

Canadian
Apple Cream Pie

Early Dutch settlers brought this recipe to Canada. Formerly only dried fruits, including dried apple slices (*Apfelschnitz*), were used because of their longer storage properties, giving it the name 'Schnitz Pie'.

8 OZ (225 G) SHORTCRUST
  PASTRY (p. 108)
1½ LB (700 G) COOKING
  APPLES
8 OZ (225 G) GRANULATED
  SUGAR
I TSP GROUND CINNAMON

2 OZ (50 G) RAISINS
I OZ (25 G) MARGARINE
4 OZ (100 G) BROWN SUGAR
¼ PT (150 ML) DOUBLE
  CREAM
MILK TO GLAZE

Roll out half the pastry and use it to line a well-greased 9 in (23 cm) pie plate. Peel, core and thickly slice the apples. Combine the sugar and cinnamon, and mix in the apples and raisins. Pile them into the pastry case and dot with margarine. Roll out the remaining pastry, cover the pie and brush with milk. Cut slits in the pastry and bake on the lowest oven shelf at 400°F (200°C, Mark 6) for 45 minutes. Remove the pie from the oven, pour the cream through the slits and bake for a further 5 minutes. Just before serving, sprinkle the pie with brown sugar and caramelize under a hot grill for 2 minutes.

Serve at once with ice-cream or yoghurt.

Alberta
Apple Honey Pie

8 OZ (225 G) SHORTCRUST
  PASTRY (p. 108)
1½ LB (700 G) COOKING
  APPLES

I TBSP CORNFLOUR
I TSP CINNAMON
½ TSP SALT
3 TBSP BROWN SUGAR

1½ OZ (40 G) BUTTER   4 OZ (100 G) CLEAR HONEY

Topping

2 OZ (50 G) BROWN SUGAR   1 OZ (25 G) BUTTER
2 OZ (50 G) CLEAR HONEY   1 OZ (25 G) CHOPPED
2 TBSP FLOUR   WALNUTS

Roll out half the pastry and line a 9 in (23 cm) well-greased pie plate with it. Peel, core and slice the apples, and place on the pastry. Mix together the cornflour, cinnamon, salt and sugar, and gradually blend them into the butter and honey. Pour this mixture over the apples. Roll out the remaining pastry, cover the pie, seal the edges and cut steam vents. Bake at 450°F (230°C, Mark 8) for 15 minutes, and then reduce the heat to 350°F (180°C, Mark 4) for a further 30 minutes. Mix together all the topping ingredients and spread over the pie. Return to the oven for a further 10 minutes.

Serve at once with ice-cream or yoghurt.

Apple
and Blackberry Hat

8 OZ (225 G) SUET PASTRY (p. 110)
2 LARGE COOKING APPLES
8 OZ (225 G) BLACKBERRIES
4 OZ (100 G) BROWN SUGAR

Divide the pastry into four pieces and roll them out into rounds. Peel, core and slice the apples and mix them with the blackberries and sugar. Lay one pastry round in the bottom of a greased 2 pt (1 l) pudding basin and cover with a third of the fruit mixture. Repeat the layers twice more and top with the last pastry round. Cover the basin with a cloth or with foil, allowing room for the pastry to rise. Tie it securely and steam for 2½ hours. Turn out carefully and serve with custard or cream.

Apple Ginger Pudding

8 OZ (225 G) SUET PASTRY (p. 110) WITH 1 TSP POWDERED
GINGER WORKED IN
1 LB (450 G) COOKING APPLES
JUICE OF 1 LEMON
4 OZ (100 G) BROWN SUGAR

Prepare the pastry and roll out as in the previous recipe. Peel and core the apples. Either dice them or cut into thick slices. Put one pastry round into the bottom of a greased 2 pt (1 l) pudding basin and add a third of the apple pieces. Sprinkle them with lemon juice and sugar and cover with another layer of pastry. Repeat these layers twice more, and then cover the basin and boil or steam the pudding for 2½–3 hours. Serve with custard or cream.

10
Hot Puddings

Coleridge holds that a man cannot have a pure mind who refuses
apple dumplings. I am not certain but he is right.

CHARLES LAMB

ooking apples, especially Bramley's Seedling and firm dessert apples like the Cox's Orange Pippin which can be stored throughout the autumn and winter, have always been a great standby in the kitchen. Besides the traditional apple pies and dumplings of the previous chapter, there are many filling and nourishing puddings in which apples form the main ingredient, and if the apples come from your own garden, the pudding has the additional merit of economy.

Boswell, in his *Life of Johnson*, mentions a sage piece of counsel given by the good doctor on this subject: 'He advised me, if possible, to have a good orchard. He knew, he said, a clergyman of small income, who brought up a family very reputably which he chiefly fed with apple dumplins.' One can visualize the large vicarage garden, full of old apple trees, and the children helping to gather and store them.

Apples seem to have been a favourite with clergymen. The previous chapter contains a recipe for Zürich Parsonage Flan, Meg Dods in her book *The Cook and Housewife's Manual* (1862) gives a recipe for 'The Manse Apple Pudding' and the diary of Parson Woodforde abounds with references to his 'Beefans' apple trees (i.e. the Norfolk Biffin) from which many a poor parishioner benefited, e.g. 'Sent poor Clarke's family a large Bushel Basket of apples to make apple dumplings for poor souls.'

The flavour of apples is extremely adaptable and several other fruits, especially apricots, pears and blackberries, can be combined with apples to vary a pudding. Indeed, a handful of blackberries picked from the hedgerow during a country walk can become the basis of a substantial pudding when added to apple purée.

Steamed Apple Pudding

8 OZ (225 G) SELF-RAISING
FLOUR
4 OZ (100 G) BROWN SUGAR
I TSP MIXED SPICE
PINCH OF SALT

2½ OZ (60 G) MARGARINE
2 EGGS
¼ PT (150 ML) MILK
I LARGE COOKING APPLE

Sift together the dry ingredients and rub in the margarine. Beat the eggs lightly and stir in with the milk. Peel, core and roughly chop the apple and add to the mixture, turn it into a well-greased 2 pt (1 l) pudding basin and steam for 2 hours.

Turn the pudding out on to a warmed plate and serve at once with cream or custard.

Apple Crumble

I LB (450 G) COOKING APPLES
6 TBSP SUGAR
I TSP CINNAMON
3 OZ (75 G) BUTTER
5 OZ (150 G) SELF-RAISING FLOUR
PINCH OF SALT

Set the oven to 400°F (200°C, Mark 6) and butter a baking dish. Peel, core and thinly slice the apples. Sprinkle with 2 tbsp of the sugar mixed with cinnamon, and pour over 2 tbsp water. Cut up 2½ oz (60 g) butter and rub into the flour until it resembles breadcrumbs, add the remaining sugar and a pinch of salt and work until the mixture clings in large lumps. Press it evenly over the apples, dot with the remaining butter and bake for 30 minutes.

Serve with cream or custard.

Blackberry and Apple Flapjack

3 OZ (75 G) BUTTER
1 TBSP SYRUP
6 OZ (175 G) ROLLED OATS
2 OZ (50 G) PLAIN FLOUR
4 OZ (100 G) DEMERARA
   SUGAR

PINCH OF SALT
1½ LB (700 G) COOKING
   APPLES
8 OZ (225 G) BLACKBERRIES
4 TBSP SUGAR
RIND AND JUICE OF ½ LEMON

Set the oven to 325°F (170°C, Mark 3) and butter a large baking dish. Put the butter and syrup in a saucepan and melt over a gentle heat; remove the pan from the heat and stir in the rolled oats, flour, demerara sugar and salt. Peel, core and slice the apples. Mix with the blackberries and put them into the dish. Sprinkle over the sugar, lemon rind and juice. Spoon the topping evenly over the fruit and bake for 1 hour.

Serve with cream or clotted cream.

Apple Crisp

You can vary this dish by mixing some blackberries with the apples, but you must then add a dessertspoon of cornflour to absorb the juices.

1 LB (450 G) COOKING APPLES
8 OZ (225 G) BROWN SUGAR
¼ TSP NUTMEG
GRATED RIND OF ½ LEMON
1 OZ (25 G) CRUSHED CORNFLAKES
4 OZ (100 G) MELTED BUTTER

Peel, core and slice the apples and put them in a deep pie dish. Sprinkle over 6 oz (175 g) of the sugar, with the nutmeg and lemon rind. Mix the remaining sugar with the cornflakes and butter. Press on top of the apples and bake at 350°F (180°C, Mark 4) for 30 minutes.

Serve with cream or yoghurt.

Eve's Pudding

1 LB (450 G) COOKING APPLES
3 OZ (75 G) GRANULATED
  SUGAR
1 TBSP CIDER
GRATED RIND OF ½ LEMON
2 OZ (50 G) BUTTER OR
  MARGARINE

2 OZ (50 G) CASTER SUGAR
1 EGG
4 OZ (100 G) SELF-RAISING
  FLOUR
1 TBSP MILK
ICING SUGAR

Set the oven to 350°F (180°C, Mark 4) and grease a deep pie dish. Peel, core and slice the apples, arrange them in the dish and sprinkle with the sugar, cider and lemon rind. Cream together the butter and caster sugar till fluffy, beat in the egg, then fold in the sifted flour with a metal spoon. Add enough milk to give a soft dropping consistency. Spread the mixture over the apples and bake for 45 minutes. Remove from the oven and dust with icing sugar.

Serve with cream or ice-cream.

Ozark Pudding

This is an American pudding, similar to the above except that 8 oz (225 g) chopped apple and 2 oz (50 g) chopped walnuts are folded into the cake mixture, which is then baked as above. Omit the granulated sugar, lemon rind and cider.

Annapolis Apple Pudding

This can also be served as a cake.

6 OZ (175 G) SELF-RAISING FLOUR	4 OZ (100 G) MARGARINE
1 TSP BAKING POWDER	1 EGG, BEATEN
PINCH OF SALT	6 FL OZ (175 ML) MILK
6 TBSP SUGAR	2 MEDIUM COOKING APPLES
	½ TSP CINNAMON

Grease an 8 in (20 cm) square cake tin.

Sift together the flour, baking powder and salt. Stir in 4 tbsp sugar and rub in the margarine. Combine the egg and milk and incorporate thoroughly. Peel, core and thickly slice the apples. Pour the batter into the cake tin and press the apple pieces partly into it. Mix the remaining sugar with the cinnamon, sprinkle over the pudding and bake at 400°F (200°C, Mark 6) for 40–45 minutes.

Serve with cream.

Pain et Pommes

4 EGGS	PINCH OF SALT
1 PT (575 ML) MILK	4 LARGE DESSERT APPLES
GRATED RIND OF 1 LEMON	A SMALL FRENCH LOAF
4 OZ (100 G) ICING SUGAR	(BATON)

Beat together the first five ingredients. Peel, core and slice the apples. Cut the bread into slices 1 in (2.5 cm) thick. Butter a pie dish and arrange in it a layer of bread, then a layer of apples. Pour half the custard mixture over this. Repeat the layers, cover the dish with aluminium foil and set it in a roasting tin half filled with cold water. Bake at 325°F (170°C, Mark 3) for 1 hour.

Serve with cream or ice-cream.

Italian Pudding

This recipe is a richer, more elaborate version of the previous one. It is adapted from Hannah Glasse's *The Art of Cookery made Plain and Easy* (1747).

4 LARGE DESSERT APPLES
4 OZ (100 G) CASTER SUGAR
GRATED RIND OF 1 ORANGE
¼ PT (150 ML) WHITE WINE
4 OZ (100 G) FRENCH BREAD
  OR LIGHT MILK LOAF

½ PT (275 ML) DOUBLE
  CREAM
4 EGGS, BEATEN
GRATED OR POWDERED
  NUTMEG

Peel, core and slice the apples. Lay them in a buttered baking dish and sprinkle with 1 oz (25 g) caster sugar and the orange rind. Pour over the wine. Break up the bread and soak it in the cream, then mash this to a pulp, add the beaten eggs and the rest of the sugar. Pour over the apples, sprinkle with nutmeg and bake at 350°F (180°C, Mark 4) for ½–¾ hour.

Apple Charlotte

> The Charlotte brown, within whose crusty sides
> A belly soft, the pulpy apple hides.

These lines, written in 1796, provide a splendid description of this pudding, which became popular in England about the same time as the name Charlotte. It may have been called after George III's queen or after the heroine of Goethe's novel *Werther*, both of whom popularized the name. There is, however, a similarity, both in name and form, to *Schaleth à la juive*, a Jewish dish. My preference is for Goethe's heroine, whose practical domesticity charmed Werther as much as her unaffected beauty. He first caught sight of her preparing supper for her younger brothers and sisters. Surely this simple, economical yet pretty dish is in keeping with her attributes.

2 LB (1 KG) APPLE PURÉE (p. 43), MADE WITH BROWN SUGAR
1 TSP MIXED SPICE
ABOUT 8 SLICES OF STALE BREAD
6 OZ (175 G) BUTTER, MELTED

Make the purée and flavour with the mixed spice. Brush a size 1 soufflé dish or deep cake tin with melted butter. Trim the crusts from the bread, dip two or three slices in the butter and use them to line the base of the dish. Halve the remaining slices, dip them in butter and arrange, overlapping, round the inside of the dish. There should be no gaps. Spoon the purée into the bread case and bake at 400°F (200°C, Mark 6) for 30 minutes. Carefully turn the charlotte out on to a plate and serve with cream.

Little Apple Dumplings

2 SMALL BREAD ROLLS
3 TBSP MILK
2 OZ (50 G) BUTTER
2 EGGS
PINCH OF SALT
8 OZ (225 G) SELF-RAISING
   FLOUR

I LB (450 G) COOKING APPLES
I OZ (25 G) BUTTER, MELTED
2 OZ (50 G) SUGAR
½ TSP CINNAMON

Soak the rolls in the milk until all the liquid is absorbed. Make a dough with the soaked rolls, butter, eggs, salt and flour. Peel and finely chop the apples and incorporate them into the dough. Form into small balls, drop them into lightly salted boiling water and cook for about 15 minutes. Lift them out with a perforated spoon, pour over the melted butter and sprinkle them with sugar and cinnamon.

Sans Souci Pudding

2 LARGE DESSERT APPLES
BUTTER FOR FRYING
2 OZ (50 G) BUTTER
1½ OZ (40 G) FLOUR
GRATED RIND OF ½ LEMON

7½ FL OZ (215 ML) MILK
2 OZ (50 G) SUGAR
I TSP VANILLA ESSENCE
3 EGGS

Peel, core and dice the apples and sauté them in a little butter. In a saucepan melt 2 oz (50 g) butter, stir in the flour and lemon rind, and

BAKING OR BOILING APPLES.

gradually add the milk. Stir over a gentle heat till the sauce thickens, remove from the heat and add the sugar and vanilla. Separate the eggs and beat the yolks into the sauce. Beat the whites until stiff and fold into the sauce along with the apples. Pour the mixture into a buttered 1½ pt (0.9 l) mould or pudding basin and steam for ¾ hour. Let it stand for 5 minutes before turning out.

Serve with cream or a hot lemon sauce.

Baked Stuffed Pippins

From *The Closet of the Eminently Learned Sir Kenelm Digby* (1669).

8 LARGE FIRM DESSERT APPLES	2 EGGS
¼ PT (150 ML) DOUBLE CREAM	1 OZ (25 G) SUGAR
	1 TSP MIXED SPICE
1 TSP SHERRY	PINCH OF SALT
2 OZ (50 G) BREADCRUMBS	MELTED BUTTER
	CASTER SUGAR

Peel the apples and slice off the tops. Core them but leave the bottom part intact so that the filling does not escape. Whip the cream and mix in the remaining ingredients. Fill the apples with this mixture and replace the tops. Brush them with melted butter, sprinkle with sugar and bake at 400°F (200°C, Mark 6) for 30 minutes.

Any leftover filling can be baked separately and served with the apples.

Apple and Curd Soufflé

3 OZ (75 G) BUTTER	GRATED RIND OF 1 LEMON
4 OZ (100 G) SUGAR	1 LB (450 G) COOKING APPLES
3 EGGS	1 OZ (25 G) BUTTER
1 LB (450 G) CURD CHEESE	

Set the oven to 425°F (220°C, Mark 7) and butter a large soufflé dish (size 3).

Cream together the first five ingredients till smooth and thoroughly blended. Peel, core and slice the apples and arrange in the base of the prepared dish. Pour over the curd mixture, dot the surface with flakes of butter and bake for 45 minutes.

Serve with cream.

Clafoutis aux Pommes

Clafoutis is a speciality of the Limousin region and consists of a thick pancake batter poured over fresh fruit. Black cherries are usually used but apples are equally good.

1 LB (450 G) DESSERT APPLES	1 TBSP RUM
2 EGGS	½ PT (275 ML) MILK
2 OZ (50 G) SUGAR	1 OZ (25 G) MELTED BUTTER
4 OZ (100 G) PLAIN FLOUR	

Peel, core and slice the apples and arrange in a shallow buttered baking dish. Beat together the eggs and sugar till thick, gradually adding the flour. When thoroughly mixed, add the remaining ingredients gradually, beating thoroughly to incorporate them. Pour the mixture over the apples and bake at 400°F (200°C, Mark 6) for 35–40 minutes.

The *clafoutis* is baked when a skewer or sharp knife inserted into the middle comes out clean.

To serve, sprinkle with sugar or icing sugar.

Apple Harvest Pudding

2 EGGS	1 LB (450 G) COOKING APPLES
4 OZ (100 G) SUGAR	1 TBSP RED JAM
4 OZ (100 G) PLAIN FLOUR	A LITTLE WATER
1 TSP BAKING POWDER	

Set the oven to 350°F (180°C, Mark 4) and grease a large soufflé dish (size 3).

Beat the eggs, add the sugar and beat till thick and light in colour. Sift together the flour and baking powder and fold into the mixture, using a metal spoon. Peel, core and thinly slice the apples. Fold them into the batter, pour into the prepared dish and bake for 1 hour. Warm the jam with a little water and serve as a sauce.

Nottingham Apple Pudding

The small Cox's Orange Pippins sold in bags in supermarkets are very suitable for this recipe.

For batter

4 OZ (100 G) PLAIN FLOUR
1 EGG
½ PT (275 ML) MILK

6 SMALL APPLES
2 OZ (50 G) BUTTER
2 OZ (50 G) BROWN SUGAR
PINCH OF MIXED SPICE,
    NUTMEG OR CINNAMON
FAT OR BUTTER

Sift the flour into a basin, make a well in the centre and crack in the egg. Add a little milk and beat, gradually drawing in all the flour. Then add the remaining milk and beat till smooth. Cover the batter and rest it for about an hour. Peel and core the apples; cream together the butter, sugar and spice. Heat the oven to 400°F (200°C, Mark 6). Put a lump of fat in a shallow baking dish or small roasting tin and heat it in the oven till bubbling. Tilt the tin to coat it with the hot fat then set the apples in it and fill each one with the butter and sugar mixture, smearing some over the top. Now pour in the prepared batter and bake the pudding for 40 minutes till risen and golden brown.

Sprinkle with sugar and serve with cream.

No good apple on a sour stock.
Proverb

Baked Apple Pudding
with Cream-cheese Sauce

The cream-cheese sauce must be made at least 2 hours in advance or even the day before to contrast with the warm baked apples.

6 OZ (175 G) CREAM CHEESE	½ TSP VANILLA ESSENCE
6 OZ (175 G) CASTER SUGAR	4–6 LARGE DESSERT APPLES
½ PT (275 ML) SINGLE CREAM	1 TBSP LEMON JUICE
	2 OZ (50 G) BUTTER

First prepare the sauce. Work the cream cheese with a wooden spoon or in a food processor till smooth. Add 4 oz (100 g) caster sugar, ¼ pt (150 ml) cream, and the vanilla essence and beat until thoroughly blended. Refrigerate for at least 2 hours before baking the apple pudding.

Peel, core and slice the apples and sprinkle them with lemon juice. Butter a 9 in (23 cm) flan dish and arrange the apple slices in it in concentric circles. Sprinkle with the remaining sugar and with flakes of butter. Bake at 400°F (200°C, Mark 6) for 30 minutes, then pour the remaining cream over the top, and increase the oven temperature to 475°F (240°C, Mark 9). Bake for a further 5 minutes. Serve warm with the cold cream-cheese sauce.

Apple and Rice Meringue

(APFELREISAUFLAUF)

3 OZ (75 G) RICE	7 TBSP SUGAR
1 PT (575 ML) MILK	JUICE OF ½ LEMON
½ OZ (10 G) BUTTER	½ STICK CINNAMON
SALT	2 EGGS
1 LB (450 G) DESSERT APPLES	

Cook the rice gently in the milk with the butter and a pinch of salt

146

until all the liquid is absorbed – this should take about 40 minutes. Let it cool. Peel, core and quarter the apples. Make a syrup with 2 tbsp sugar, 6 tbsp water, the lemon juice and cinnamon and cook the apple pieces in this till soft. Mix the egg yolks and 2 tbsp sugar with the rice and put into a buttered baking dish. Lift out the apples with a slotted spoon and arrange them on the rice. Whisk the egg whites with a pinch of salt till stiff, and then beat in the rest of the sugar. Spread this meringue over the apples and bake at 400°F (200°C, Mark 6) for 20 minutes.

Another method is to peel and core the apples, leaving them whole, cook them in the syrup, and then press them into the meringue topping and fill them with jam. Bake in the same way as above.

Serve with cream.

Baked Apple and Almond Pudding

4 OZ (100 G) GROUND ALMONDS
4 OZ (100 G) SUGAR
2 LB (1 KG) UNSWEETENED APPLE PURÉE (p. 43)
3 EGGS
GRATED RIND AND JUICE OF 1 LEMON
2 TBSP CORNFLOUR

Mix the ground almonds with the sugar. Stir half this mixture into the apple purée and put it into a buttered baking dish.

Separate the eggs and beat the yolks with the remaining almond and sugar mixture, the lemon rind and juice and cornflour. Whisk the whites till stiff and fold them into the mixture. Spread over the apple purée and bake at 350°F (180°C, Mark 4) for 40 minutes. Serve with cream or custard.

An apple may happen to be better given than eaten
Thomas Fuller, 'Gnomologia'

Malvern Pudding

½ PT (275 ML) MILK

1 ROUNDED TBSP CORNFLOUR

2 EGGS, BEATEN

4 OZ (100 G) SUGAR

1 LB (450 G) APPLE PURÉE (p. 43)

1 OZ (25 G) DEMERARA SUGAR (OPTIONAL)

Put 2 tbsp milk in a bowl with the cornflour and mix to a smooth paste. Bring the rest of the milk to the boil, pour it on to the cornflour paste and amalgamate the two; then return the mixture to the pan and stir till it thickens. Remove the pan from the heat and gradually blend in the beaten eggs and the sugar.

Put the apple purée in the base of a buttered baking dish and pour the custard over it. Bake at 400°F (200°C, Mark 6) for 25 minutes.

As a finishing touch, sprinkle 1 oz (25 g) demerara sugar over the custard and brown quickly under a hot grill.

Serve with cream.

Apple Fritters
or Beignets aux Pommes

This has been a popular recipe for centuries. The earliest English cookery book, *The Form of Cury* (1390) gives a recipe for 'Apple and Pasternak (water parsnip) Fritters', in which the batter was made from eggs, flour, ale and saffron, and the fritter was dipped in almond milk. Hannah Glasse, writing in 1770, gives a recipe using 8 egg yolks, 4 egg whites, a quart of cream, a pint of sack (sherry) and ¾ pint of ale! In the nineteenth century a simpler version evolved.

The apples can be soaked in rum or brandy before they are dipped in the batter; however, the disadvantage of this method is that the batter does not adhere so well to the soaked fruit, so it must be dipped in flour first. Another method is to grate the apples (cf. Cheesy Apple Bacon

Fritters, p. 78) and soak them, along with raisins, in alcohol, fold them into the batter and fry spoonfuls of it in the hot fat.

7 OZ (200 G) PLAIN FLOUR	I TBSP RUM
PINCH OF SALT	FAT FOR FRYING
2 EGGS, SEPARATED	A LITTLE EXTRA FLOUR
½ PT (275 ML) MILK	4 LARGE DESSERT APPLES
4 TBSP SUGAR	½ TSP CINNAMON

Sift the flour and salt into a basin, add the egg yolks and some milk. Beat, gradually drawing in the liquid and adding the remaining milk. When smooth, beat in 2 tbsp sugar and the rum. At this point the batter can be rested for about an hour.

Whisk the egg whites till stiff and fold into the batter. Peel and core the apples, and slice into ¼ in (½ cm) rounds.

Melt the fat in a frying-pan, and when it is really hot, dip the apple slices into the extra flour and then into the batter and fry till golden brown and crisp. Mix the cinnamon with the remaining sugar and sprinkle over the fritters. Serve at once.

Apple Tansy

Another old favourite, this recipe is no longer flavoured by the bitter herb which gives it its name but by a delicious combination of spices and rosewater, typical of seventeenth-century cookery.

4 EGGS, SEPARATED	I TSP ROSEWATER
¼ PT (150 ML) DOUBLE	I LB (450 G) DESSERT APPLES
CREAM	2 OZ (50 G) BUTTER
PINCH OF NUTMEG	
PINCH OF CINNAMON	*To serve*
PINCH OF GROUND GINGER	SUGAR
4 OZ (100 G) CASTER SUGAR	GRATED ORANGE RIND

Beat together the egg yolks, cream, spices, sugar and rosewater, until smooth. Whisk the whites till stiff and fold into the mixture. Peel, core and slice the apples and fold them in. Melt the butter in a frying-pan and pour in the mixture. Fry for about 6 minutes, or until the underside is set and golden brown. Then put the pan under a hot grill for 2–3 minutes. Serve sprinkled with sugar and grated orange rind.

Apples in the Alps

4 FIRM DESSERT APPLES	2 EGG WHITES
2 TBSP RED JAM OR JELLY	PINCH OF SALT
2 TBSP SUGAR	3 TBSP ICING SUGAR
JUICE OF ½ LEMON	3 TBSP GROUND ALMONDS
½ OZ (10 G) BUTTER	

Peel, halve and core the apples and lay, rounded side up, on a flat ovenproof dish. Warm together the jam, sugar and lemon juice. Brush the apples with this, reserving one teaspoonful, put a little butter on each one and bake at 400°F (200°C, Mark 6) for 20 minutes. Meanwhile, whisk together the egg whites and salt until stiff and fold in the reserved jam sauce, the sieved icing sugar and the ground almonds. Put this mixture into a forcing bag with a rose nozzle and pipe rosettes of meringue among the apples. Return to the oven for 5 minutes.

Serve with cream or ice-cream.

Brown Betty

Any type of apple is suitable for this recipe.

6 SLICES WHOLEMEAL BREAD
2 OZ (50 G) BUTTER
1½ LB (700 G) APPLES
2 OZ (50 G) BROWN SUGAR
GRATED RIND AND JUICE OF 1 LEMON
3 TBSP GOLDEN SYRUP OR HONEY

Butter the bread generously and cut each slice into four pieces. Peel, core and slice the apples. Arrange a layer of bread in a buttered baking dish, cover with half the apples, half the sugar and some lemon rind and juice. Repeat these layers and then top with the remaining bread. Warm together the syrup (or honey) and 2 tbsp water. Pour over the pudding and bake at 350°F (180°C, Mark 4) for 45 minutes.

Serve with cream or custard.

Crêpes aux Pommes

Batter	Filling
4 OZ (100 G) PLAIN FLOUR	8 OZ (225 G) DESSERT APPLES
2 EGGS	4 WALNUTS
1 DESSERTSPOON OLIVE OIL	GRATED RIND OF 1 ORANGE
½ PT (275 ML) MILK	1 TBSP RUM
2 OZ (50 G) MELTED BUTTER	A LITTLE EXTRA BUTTER
1 TBSP CASTER SUGAR	ICING SUGAR

Sift the flour into a bowl, make a well in it for the eggs and oil and beat until all the flour is absorbed. Gradually add the milk, beating constantly, then the melted butter and sugar. Set aside while you prepare the filling.

Peel and grate the apples and chop the walnuts finely. Mix with the orange rind and rum.

Heat a little butter in a pancake or omelette pan and pour in enough pancake batter to cover the bottom. Cook until firm underneath, then flip over and cook the other side. Slide the pancake on to a plate, put a tablespoonful of apple mixture in the middle and roll it up. Continue in this way until the batter and filling are used up. Sprinkle the pancakes with icing sugar.

Blackcaps

This simple recipe was very popular in the seventeenth century.

Today it is almost unknown, although it is much simpler and quicker than any baked apple recipe.

6 LARGE FIRM DESSERT APPLES
RIND AND JUICE OF 1 LEMON
2 TBSP ORANGE-FLOWER WATER
1 TBSP WHITE OR RED WINE
4 OZ (100 G) SUGAR
1 TSP CINNAMON (OPTIONAL)

Core and halve the unpeeled apples and lay them, cut side downwards, in a roasting tin. Grate the lemon rind and squeeze the juice. Combine these and add the orange-flower water and wine. (Red wine results in a lovely pink syrup.) Pour this mixture over the apple halves and sprinkle them with sugar. (If using cinnamon, mix it with the sugar.) Bake at 400°F (200°C, Mark 6) for about 30 minutes, by which time the apples should be soft, coated in crisp sugar and surrounded by a delicious sharp-flavoured syrup. To live up to the name, pass the dish under a hot grill to caramelize the sugar.

Serve with cream.

Baked Apples

This very simple and popular method of baking apples has so many variations that a precise recipe would be inappropriate. The unpeeled cooking apples should be washed, dried and cored, and a cut made round the middle to prevent them from bursting during the cooking time. They may be stuffed simply with brown or white sugar, or some dried fruit and/or nuts may also be added, and some extra flavouring, if desired. A little grated orange or lemon rind is especially good. Some fresh fruits are suitable, especially mashed bananas and blackberries which contrast nicely in flavour and texture. Any of these fillings can also be flavoured with honey, jam, fruit juice, sherry, brandy – in fact, the list is endless.

Arrange the apples in a shallow ovenproof dish and make sure they are not touching each other. Top each one with a small piece of butter and add a little water (fruit juice or sherry, etc.) to the dish. This reduces during cooking and becomes a delicious syrup.

Bake the apples at 350°F (180°C, Mark 4) for about 45 minutes.

Baked apples can be very quickly cooked in a microwave oven. Prepare as above, cover with clingfilm and bake for 1½ minutes per apple.

The following four recipes are examples of interesting variations on the baked apple.

Green Caps

After baking the apples with your chosen filling, you can decorate them in the manner suggested by John Farley in his book *The London Art of Cookery* (1783). 'Brush the apples with oil, sprinkle with sugar, and replace in the oven until they sparkle. Serve in custard and stick single flowers in every apple.'

Swedish Baked Apples

2 OZ (50 G) GROUND ALMONDS
1 OZ (25 G) CASTER SUGAR
1 EGG WHITE
4 LARGE COOKING APPLES
2 OZ (50 G) MELTED BUTTER
1 OZ (25 G) FINE BREADCRUMBS

Mix the almonds, sugar, 1 tbsp water and the unbeaten egg white to a smooth paste. Peel the apples and core, leaving the bottom part intact. Brush with the melted butter and coat with the breadcrumbs. Stand the apples in a baking dish or tin. They must not touch each other. Fill with the almond paste and bake at 350°F (180°C, Mark 4) for 40 minutes.

Pommes Vesuve

1 OZ (25 G) RAISINS
4 TBSP RUM
4 COOKING APPLES
1 OZ (25 G) WALNUTS
4 TBSP HONEY
2 OZ (50 G) BUTTER

Warm the raisins in 1 tbsp rum over a gentle heat until plump. Prepare the apples as for baked apples. Chop the walnuts and combine with the raisins and honey. Stuff each apple with this mixture and top with a lump of butter. Put the apples in an ovenproof dish and bake for 45 minutes at 350°F (180°C, Mark 4). When ready to serve, warm the remaining rum, pour over the apples and flambé.

German Baked Apples with Foamy Wine Sauce

These may be served with cream, or with the following sauce, which is rather similar to zabaglione. An electric mixer or blender is a great help.

4 COOKING APPLES
JUICE OF ½ LEMON
4 OZ (100 G) GLACÉ CHERRIES
2 TBSP GROUND ALMONDS

FLAKED ALMONDS
1 OZ (25 G) BUTTER
1 TBSP SUGAR
1 WINEGLASS WHITE WINE

Peel and core the apples. Set them in a shallow dish and pour the lemon juice over them. Finely chop the cherries, blend with the ground almonds to a paste and stuff the apples with this. Stick some flaked almonds into the flesh of the apples. Put a knob of butter on each apple, sprinkle with sugar and pour over the wine and a glass of water. Bake at 350°F (180°C, Mark 4) for about 40 minutes.

Foamy wine sauce

2 EGGS
I TBSP LEMON JUICE
½ PT (275 ML) WHITE WINE
2½ OZ (60 G) SUGAR
I TSP CORNFLOUR

Beat the eggs thoroughly. Gradually add the lemon juice and wine, beating constantly, then the sugar and cornflour. Put the sauce in the top of a double boiler or in a pan over boiling water, and stir constantly till it is thick. Do not let it boil.

Chinese Toffee-apple Fritters
(BA TSU PING GUO)

This recipe is less complicated than it sounds, but it must be served immediately.

Batter

3 OZ (75 G) PLAIN FLOUR
PINCH OF SALT
I EGG
I TBSP GROUNDNUT OIL

4 DESSERT APPLES

I LARGE BOTTLE
GROUNDNUT OIL

Caramel

8 OZ (225 G) CASTER SUGAR
I TBSP GROUNDNUT OIL
I OZ (25 G) SESAME SEEDS

Blend the batter ingredients with 2 tbsp water and beat until thick. Peel and core the apples and cut into thick slices. Dip them in the batter and deep-fry in the oil till golden. This only takes 1–2 minutes. Lift them out with a slotted spoon on to kitchen paper and keep them warm while you prepare the caramel.

Over a gentle heat dissolve the sugar in the oil and ¼ pt (150 ml) water, and then turn up the heat and cook to a pale golden caramel. Have ready a container full of boiling water and stand the pan in it to keep the caramel liquid. Dip the fritters into it, turning to coat completely. Sprinkle them with sesame seeds. Serve at once.

And finally, two very quick but sophisticated French desserts, ideal for a special lunch.

Omelette Normande

1½ OZ (40 G) BUTTER

3 DESSERT APPLES
(PREFERABLY RUSSETS OR
COX'S)

2 TBSP CASTER SUGAR

GRATED RIND OF ½ ORANGE

I TBSP CALVADOS

3 EGGS

A LITTLE ICING SUGAR

Melt 1 oz (25 g) butter in a saucepan. Peel, core and slice the apples and add to the butter with 1 tbsp sugar and the orange rind. Cook over a very gentle heat for 10 minutes, or until the apples are soft but unbroken. Add the calvados, and cover and set aside, but keep warm.

Separate the eggs. Beat the yolks with the rest of the sugar. Whisk the whites till stiff and fold into the yolk mixture.

Melt ½ oz (10 g) butter in an omelette pan and pour in the mixture. Cook over a gentle heat for 3–5 minutes, and then put it under a hot grill for 1–2 minutes. (Watch it carefully as it can burn very readily.) Spoon the apple filling and juices on to one side of the omelette and fold the other side over it. Dust sparingly with sifted icing sugar.

For a professional finish, heat a skewer under the grill and score the omelette in a criss-cross pattern.

Bananas Brûlées

4 RIPE BANANAS

4 TBSP WHIPPED CREAM

I LB (450 G) APPLE PURÉE (p. 43)

4 OZ (100 G) MELTED BUTTER

4 TBSP CASTER SUGAR

Cut a long slit in the skin of each banana and carefully press out the flesh. Fold the cream into the apple purée and fill the banana skins with this mixture. Slice the banana flesh and arrange on top of the apple purée. Arrange the bananas in a grill pan, dribble melted butter over them and sprinkle with sugar. Brown quickly under a hot grill and serve at once.

Strata jacent passim sua quaeque sub arbore poma.
(Beneath each tree its fruit lies strewn around
or The apples lie scattered here and there, each under its own tree.)

Virgil, *Eclogues*

11
Cold Puddings

I will make an end of my dinner, there's pippins and cheese to come.

SHAKESPEARE,
Merry Wives of Windsor

n general, cold desserts are associated with summer fruits. Fruit which ripens in autumn coincides with colder temperatures, when light meals are beginning to be replaced by more substantial ones. The very phrase 'apple pudding' conjures up the idea of a hot, filling, perhaps even stodgy dish. But the versatile apple is just as much at home in the chilled cheesecake, mousse, ice-cream or fruit salad as in the pie and dumpling.

The simplest cold apple dessert, the fruit itself, has always been popular. In 1502 at a banquet in the town-hall of Lübeck, the menu consisted of elk ham, boiled venison, sturgeon and apples.

> For wafers, spic'd cakes, tart and custard,
> For apples, carawaies and cheese . . .

runs an Elizabethan grace, after listing the main courses. This, and the Shakespeare quotation above, show how esteemed apples were at that time.

In 1825 Brillat-Savarin wrote in *La Physiologie du Goût* of dinner with the *curé*, 'In its turn, dessert came. It consisted of some Semoncel cheese, three Calville apples and a pot of jam.' And of course we still enjoy apples served simply with cheese and wine or on their own.

On the whole, however, the Elizabethans liked to cook their fruit and vegetables. With a few exceptions they considered raw fare unwholesome, so apple pies, tarts and tansies were popular, while 'codlins and cream' was the forerunner of the fruit fool.

The texture of cold apple purée is well adapted to blend with cream, custard, gelatine, etc. The fresh fruit sliced makes a pretty salad ingredient or decoration, but it must be dipped in lemon juice or syrup to preserve its whiteness.

Codlins and Cream

A well-known Elizabethan dish. The name is also given by country folk to the great willowherb. The recipes of the sixteenth and seventeenth centuries are remarkably consistent in their flavourings of mace and rosewater, and they also include a grain of ambergris! Grated orange or lemon rind, or bruised root ginger are acceptable alternative flavourings.

2 EGG YOLKS
½ PT (275 ML) DOUBLE CREAM
1 TBSP SUGAR
1 BLADE OF MACE
2 TSP ROSEWATER
1 LB (450 G) APPLE PURÉE (p. 43)

Beat the egg yolks into the cream, add the sugar, mace and rosewater and stir over a gentle heat until the custard thickens. Then remove the pan from the heat and let the custard cool. When cold, mix it with the apple purée. Serve with sponge fingers or crisp biscuits.

Apple,
Rum and Raisin Mousse

4 OZ (100 G) RAISINS	8 OZ (225 G) CURD CHEESE
2 TBSP RUM	½ OZ (10 G) GELATINE
1½ LB (700 G) APPLE PURÉE (p. 43)	2 EGG WHITES
	CREAM
GRATED RIND OF ½ ORANGE	1 DESSERT APPLE
2 OZ (50 G) HONEY	1 TBSP LEMON JUICE
2 OZ (50 G) BROWN SUGAR	

Warm the raisins and rum over a gentle heat till plump. Combine the warm apple purée, orange rind, honey and brown sugar. Stir the curd cheese with a wooden spoon till soft and blend in. Soften the gelatine in 1 tbsp water and warm till it dissolves. Stir it into the mixture with the raisins and rum and leave to cool. Whip the egg whites till stiff and fold in.

Pour the mixture into a soufflé dish or bowl. When set, decorate with cream and slices of dessert apple brushed with lemon juice.

Apple and Blackberry Fool

I LB (450 G) COOKING APPLES
8 OZ (225 G) BLACKBERRIES
JUICE OF ½ LEMON
4 OZ (100 G) BROWN SUGAR
½ PT (275 ML) WHIPPING CREAM
I TBSP BRANDY OR CALVADOS (OPTIONAL)

Peel, core and slice the apples and put them in a pan with the blackberries and lemon juice. Cover and cook over a very gentle heat until the fruit is soft; then rub it through a sieve, add the brown sugar and leave to cool.

Whip the cream until thick and light but not stiff. Carefully fold it into the fruit purée and add the brandy or calvados if desired. Pour into a glass bowl or individual glasses, and chill. Serve with sponge fingers or *langue de chat* biscuits.

Baked Apple Custard

I OZ (25 G) BUTTER   2 EGGS
2 TBSP ICING SUGAR   ¼ PT (150 ML) MILK
PINCH OF CINNAMON   2 TSP CORNFLOUR
I TBSP RAISINS   I OZ (25 G) FLAKED ALMONDS
6 FIRM DESSERT APPLES

Melt the butter in a frying-pan and stir in the icing sugar, cinnamon and raisins. Peel and core the apples and slice them into fine rounds. Lay them in the frying-pan and cook over a very gentle heat until they are golden and soft. Butter a soufflé dish and transfer the apples and raisins to it. Beat together the eggs, milk and cornflour and strain this mixture over the apples. Sprinkle on the flaked almonds and bake at 400°F (200°C, Mark 6) for 30 minutes. Serve hot or cold with cream.

Apple Cheesecake

Base

8 OZ (225 G) DIGESTIVE
  BISCUITS
2 OZ (50 G) BUTTER
1 TBSP GOLDEN SYRUP

Filling

8 OZ (225 G) CURD CHEESE
6 OZ (175 G) CASTER SUGAR
1 SMALL CAN EVAPORATED
  MILK

8 OZ (225 G) UNSWEETENED
  APPLE PURÉE (p. 43)
2 EGGS

To decorate

2 DESSERT APPLES
APRICOT OR APPLE JELLY
  GLAZE
FLAKED ALMONDS
  (OPTIONAL)

Crush the biscuits with a rolling-pin. Melt the butter with the syrup, stir in the crumbs and press into the base of an 8½ in (21 cm) spring-clip tin.

Blend together the curd cheese, sugar, evaporated milk, apple purée and the egg yolks. Whisk the whites till stiff and fold into the mixture. Pour on to the biscuit base and bake at 325°F (170°C, Mark 3) for 30 minutes. Turn off the oven, open the door a little and leave the cheesecake to cool for about an hour.

When the cheesecake is cold, peel, core and slice the apples and arrange on the top. Cover them with the glaze and sprinkle with some flaked almonds if desired.

Année venteuse, année pommeuse.
(Windy year, year rich in apples)
French proverb

Apple
and Blackberry Cheesecake

Base

8 OZ (225 G) DIGESTIVE
  BISCUITS
2 OZ (50 G) BUTTER

Filling

1 LB (450 G) APPLE PURÉE
  (p. 43)
¼ PT (150 ML) WHIPPING
  CREAM

8 OZ (225 G) CREAM CHEESE
4 OZ (100 G) GRANULATED
  SUGAR
8 OZ (225 G) BLACKBERRIES
4 OZ (100 G) DEMERARA
  SUGAR

Crush the biscuits with a rolling-pin. Melt the butter and stir in the biscuit crumbs until the butter is absorbed. Press into the base and up the sides of an 8½ in (21 cm) spring-clip tin and put it in the fridge to harden.

Fill the biscuit base with cold apple purée. Whip the cream lightly. Work the cream cheese till soft, beat in the granulated sugar and fold in the cream. Spoon over the apple purée. Arrange the blackberries on the top, sprinkle with demerara sugar and put under a hot grill just long enough for the sugar to melt. Put in the fridge for several hours.

Canadian Apple Torte

2 OZ (50 G) BUTTER
5 OZ (150 G) SUGAR
VANILLA ESSENCE
4 OZ (100 G) PLAIN FLOUR
8 OZ (225 G) FULL-FAT
  CREAM CHEESE

4 OZ (100 G) CASTER SUGAR
1 EGG
1 LB (450 G) COOKING APPLES
½ TSP CINNAMON
1 OZ (25 G) FLAKED ALMONDS

Cream the butter, half the sugar and a few drops of vanilla essence, then blend in the flour and pat into the bottom of a 9 in (23 cm) spring-clip tin. Bake at 350°F (180°C, Mark 4) for 10 minutes.

Meanwhile beat the cream cheese and caster sugar till smooth. Beat in the egg and a little vanilla essence and pour over the biscuit base. Peel, core and slice the apples. Combine the remaining sugar with the cinnamon and toss the apple slices in this mixture. Spoon them over the cream-cheese layer and sprinkle with the almonds. Bake at 450°F (230°C, Mark 8) for 10 minutes. Reduce the heat to 400°F (200°C, Mark 6) and bake for a further 25 minutes. Loosen the *torte* from the rim of the tin and cool before removing.

Iced Apples
with Jam Sauce

4 FIRM DESSERT APPLES
4 OZ (100 G) SUGAR
½ PT (275 ML) WHITE WINE
JUICE OF ½ LEMON
2 TBSP RED JAM OR JELLY
VANILLA ICE-CREAM

Peel the apples, slice a 'lid' off the top of each and then core them. Dissolve the sugar in ¼ pt (150 ml) water and boil for 2 minutes. Add the wine and lemon juice, and gently poach the apples, plus lids, for about 15 minutes in this syrup. Let them cool in the syrup, lift out with a perforated spoon into individual glass dishes and chill. Warm the jam or jelly until it becomes runny and add the syrup gradually.

Just before serving, fill each apple with ice-cream – the corer will lift out portions which fit exactly. Cover the apples with their lids, pour over the hot sauce and serve at once.

Apple Bavarois

I LB (450 G) UNSWEETENED APPLE PURÉE (p. 43)	5 TBSP CIDER
	¼ PT (150 ML) YOGHURT
4 OZ (100 G) CLEAR HONEY	¼ PT (150 ML) SINGLE CREAM
2 TBSP GELATINE	2 EGGS

Liquidize the purée or rub it through a sieve. Add the honey and stir till well blended. Sprinkle the gelatine over the cider, and when absorbed, heat gently till dissolved. Beat together the yoghurt, single cream and egg yolks. Add the sieved apple purée and blend well. Beat in the gelatine. Leave until the mixture is on the point of setting and then whisk the egg whites until stiff. Fold into the mixture, pour into a mould or glass dish and leave to set in the fridge for several hours, preferably overnight.

Scandinavian Apple Cake

This is a simple pudding, similar to the English Brown Betty and Apple Charlotte. All Scandinavian countries lay claim to it: in Norway it is known as *Tilelorte Bondepiker*, in Sweden as *Appelkaka*, and in Denmark as *Aeblekage*. It can be served hot or cold with a variety of jams, with vanilla sauce, or with whipped cream and grated chocolate, as in this version. If possible, serve it in a glass dish so that the layers are visible.

I ½ LB (700 G) APPLE PURÉE (p. 43)	6 OZ (175 G) COARSE BREADCRUMBS
GRATED RIND OF ½ LEMON	I OZ (25 G) SUGAR
3 OZ (75 G) BUTTER	WHIPPED CREAM
	GRATED CHOCOLATE

Prepare the apple purée, stir in the grated lemon rind and let it cool. Melt the butter in a pan and fry the crumbs till brown and crisp. Add the sugar and leave to cool. Arrange the purée and crumbs in layers in a glass dish or soufflé dish, finishing with a layer of crumbs, and decorate with swirls of whipped cream and grated chocolate.

Charlotte aux Pommes with Sabayon Sauce

Charlotte

2 LB (1 KG) COOKING APPLES
6 OZ (175 G) CASTER SUGAR
A FEW DROPS VANILLA
   ESSENCE
½ PT (275 ML) SWEET CIDER
1 TBSP CALVADOS
1 OZ (25 G) BUTTER
½ OZ (10 G) GELATINE
1 PACKET SPONGE FINGERS

Sauce

3 EGG YOLKS
4 OZ (100 G) CASTER SUGAR
¼ PT (150 ML) CIDER
1 DESSERTSPOON CALVADOS

Peel, core and slice the apples. Put them in a pan with the sugar, vanilla essence and half the cider. Cook until the apples are soft, remove half the mixture and mash the remainder till smooth. Continue to cook over a gentle heat, stirring frequently, until the purée is thick. Stir in half the calvados and the butter. Soak the gelatine in a little hot water and add, stirring till it dissolves. Now stir in the rest of the apple mixture.

Butter a charlotte tin or medium soufflé dish. Mix the rest of the cider and calvados and soak the sponge fingers in it; then arrange them around the sides and bottom of the tin. Pour in the apple mixture, cover with any remaining sponge fingers and place a plate and a heavy weight on top. Chill thoroughly, preferably overnight.

To make the sauce, beat together the egg yolks and sugar until the mixture is thick enough to leave a trail. Add the cider and calvados, and place the bowl over a gentle heat (or in a bain marie). Continue beating till you have a light foamy mixture. Cool and serve with the unmoulded charlotte.

Apple Grütz

A popular pudding in Germany and Scandinavia, *Grütz* is usually made with red fruits, hence its Danish name *Rødgrød*.

1 LB (450 G) DESSERT APPLES
½ PT (275 ML) WHITE WINE
½ PT (275 ML) APPLE OR
   ORANGE JUICE
6 OZ (175 G) SUGAR

½ VANILLA POD
RIND OF 1 LEMON
2 OZ (50 G) RAISINS
3 OZ (75 G) CORNFLOUR
2 TBSP LEMON JUICE

Peel, core and slice the apples. Put the wine, fruit juice, sugar, bruised vanilla pod, lemon rind and raisins in a pan and heat gently till the sugar dissolves, then poach the apples in this syrup for 10 minutes. Remove the pod and rind. Lift out the apples with a slotted spoon and put them in a glass dish. Measure out ½ pt (275 ml) water, mix a little of it with the cornflour to form a paste, add the remaining water and pour into the pan. Bring to the boil, and, when thickened, add the lemon juice. Cool slightly and pour over the apples. Serve cold with cream.

Apple, Mint and Yoghurt Ice

1 LB (450 G) COOKING APPLES
A GOOD HANDFUL OF MINT
2 TBSP HONEY
2 EGGS
¼ PT (150 ML) NATURAL YOGHURT

Peel, core and slice the apples. Cook them with the mint and 2 tbsp water until soft. Sieve the resulting purée and beat in the honey, egg yolks and yoghurt. Freeze till mushy. Whisk the egg whites till stiff. Fold into the mixture and freeze till firm.

Calvados Sorbet

8 OZ (225 G) CASTER SUGAR
1 LB (450 G) DESSERT APPLES
RIND AND JUICE OF 1 LEMON
3 TBSP CALVADOS
1 EGG WHITE

Put the sugar in a pan with ½ pt (275 ml) water and heat gently until the sugar dissolves. Peel, core and slice the apples and add to the pan along with the finely pared lemon rind and juice. Poach the apples in the syrup until soft and then remove the rind. Liquidize the apples and syrup until very smooth, pour into a plastic tray and freeze till slushy.

Take out the mixture, add the calvados and beat till it is smooth and any ice crystals have broken down. Whisk the egg white till it stands in peaks and fold it in. Re-freeze the sorbet.

Apple Meringue Topping

This recipe can be used as a cake topping, as an accompaniment to a pudding, or simply served on its own with sponge fingers. However, it must be eaten on the day it is made.

1 EGG WHITE
2 OZ (50 G) CASTER SUGAR
1 DESSERT APPLE
A LITTLE COCHINEAL (optional)

Whisk the egg white till stiff and fold in the sugar. Peel and grate the apple and fold in, along with a few drops of cochineal, if desired.

12
Cakes and Confectionery

There was cakes and apples
in all the chapels.

R. H. BARHAM,
'Barney Maquire's Account of the Coronation'

lthough apples have always been a popular ingredient in the pies and puddings of British cookery, they feature much less frequently in cakes. It is not really surprising that the two English cake recipes in this section are from Dorset and Devonshire; both areas where the fruit is so plentiful that the recipes may well have originated from necessity.

On the continent, much more frequent use is made of fresh fruit in baking. This is especially true in Germany where apples, pears and plums are used in a variety of cakes and tea-breads, sometimes as a filling, sometimes for decoration. In Denmark, apple filling is often used in the mouth-watering pastries.

But the majority of these recipes originated in Europe and travelled with early settlers to the New World, where they have become part of the great tradition of American and Canadian baking. A popular American idea is the 'pudding cake' served with coffee at lunch time. Chocolate Apple-sauce Cake, Penticton Chiffon Cake and American Apple and Walnut Cake are delicious examples.

Other recipes in this chapter owe their origins to medieval fairs and markets. These 'fairings' include Toffee Apples, Oliebollen and Parisian Gingerbread.

Spicy
Apple Crumble Bars

Any variety of apple may be used in this Canadian recipe.

Crumble	Filling
6 OZ (175 G) BUTTER	1½ LB (700 G) APPLES
8 OZ (225 G) BROWN SUGAR	2 OZ (50 G) GRANULATED
6 OZ (175 G) PLAIN FLOUR	SUGAR
I TSP BAKING POWDER	2 TBSP CORNFLOUR
½ TSP SALT	8 OZ (225 G) RAISINS
4 OZ (100 G) PORRIDGE OATS	2 TSP CINNAMON
	½ TSP GROUND NUTMEG
	½ TSP GROUND ALLSPICE
	I OZ (25 G) BUTTER

Work the butter and sugar together till the mixture forms large crumbs, then work in the other crumble ingredients. Pat half this mixture into a well-buttered 13 × 9 in (33 × 23 cm) swiss-roll tin, pressing it down evenly with the back of a spoon.

Peel, core and grate the apples and mix with the sugar, cornflour, raisins and spices. Spread this mixture over the base and top evenly with the remaining crumble. Dot with flakes of butter and bake at 350°F (180°C, Mark 4) for 45 minutes. Cool and cut into bars.

Chocolate
Apple-sauce Cake

This cake keeps very well.

2 OZ (50 G) RAISINS	½ TSP CINNAMON
2 OZ (50 G) STONED CHOPPED	½ TSP GROUND CLOVES
DATES	½ TSP GROUND ALLSPICE

½ TSP GROUND NUTMEG

8 OZ (225 G) PLAIN FLOUR

I TSP BAKING POWDER

½ TSP SALT

2 TBSP COCOA POWDER

12 OZ (350 G) CASTER SUGAR

I LB (450 G) UNSWEETENED
    APPLE PURÉE (p. 43)

4 OZ (100 G) BUTTER

2 EGGS

2 OZ (50 G) CHOPPED
    WALNUTS

Butter a 9 in (23 cm) square cake tin, line the base with greaseproof paper, and grease this too.

Put the raisins, dates, spices and ¼ pt (150 ml) water in a saucepan, stir well, bring to the boil and then leave to cool. Drain, reserving the liquid. Sift together the flour, baking powder, salt and cocoa powder. Add the sugar and beat in the apple purée, butter and the reserved liquid. Add the eggs and beat for 2 minutes. Stir in the raisins, dates and walnuts. Pour the mixture into the greased cake tin and bake at 350°F (180°C, Mark 4) for 50–60 minutes. Ice with mocha icing.

Mocha Icing

2 OZ (50 G) PLAIN CHOCOLATE

I TBSP BLACK COFFEE

I EGG, BEATEN

4 OZ (100 G) ICING SUGAR

Melt the chocolate and coffee in a small pan over gently simmering water. Remove from the heat and beat in the egg; then gradually add the icing sugar and blend well.

With a heart that is true,
I'll be waiting for you
In the shade of the old apple tree.
Harry Williams (1905)

Dorset Apple Cake

This cake is eaten hot.

2 LARGE COOKING APPLES	2 OZ (50 G) CURRANTS
2 OZ (50 G) BUTTER	2 EGGS, BEATEN
4 OZ (100 G) SELF-RAISING	BROWN SUGAR, BUTTER AND
FLOUR	EXTRA CASTER SUGAR
4 OZ (100 G) CASTER SUGAR	

Set the oven to 375°F (190°C, Mark 5) and grease a 7½ in (19 cm) square cake tin. Peel and finely chop the apples. Cut the butter into small pieces and, using your fingertips, rub it into the flour. Stir in the chopped apples, caster sugar and currants. Gradually incorporate the eggs and blend to a smooth dough. Turn it into the prepared cake tin and bake for ¾ hour or until a skewer inserted into the cake comes out clean.

Turn the cake out on to a hot dish, split it horizontally and butter the lower layer. Sprinkle it generously with brown sugar, replace the top and sprinkle it with caster sugar. Serve immediately.

German Apple Cake

4 OZ (100 G) BUTTER	*Topping*
4 OZ (100 G) CASTER SUGAR	4–6 SMALL DESSERT APPLES
2 LARGE EGGS	1 TSP GELATINE
A FEW DROPS LEMON	1–2 DESSERTSPOONS
FLAVOURING	APRICOT JAM
8 OZ (225 G) PLAIN FLOUR	ICING SUGAR
2 TSP BAKING POWDER	
1 DESSERTSPOON MILK	

Set the oven to 350°F (180°C, Mark 4) and grease an 8½ in (21 cm) spring-clip or loose-bottomed cake tin. Cream the butter and sugar till fluffy, and whisk in the eggs and lemon flavouring. Sift together the flour and baking powder and fold in. Finally stir in enough milk, about a dessertspoon, to achieve a smooth cake mixture. Pour into the prepared cake tin. Peel, quarter and core the apples. Score the rounded sides and arrange them in a pattern on top of the cake. Bake for 50–55 minutes.

Meanwhile, prepare the glaze. Sprinkle the gelatine over 2 dessert-spoons hot water. When soft, add the jam and stir over a gentle heat till dissolved. Remove the hot cake from the oven and brush at once with the glaze. Dust liberally with sifted icing sugar.

Mecklenburg Apple Cake

This cake is sometimes made as a pie in a deep pastry case.

Base

4 OZ (100 G) BUTTER
4 OZ (100 G) CASTER SUGAR
2 EGGS
6 OZ (175 G) SELF-RAISING
   FLOUR

Filling

1 LB (450 G) COOKING APPLES
GRATED RIND AND JUICE OF
   ½ LEMON
3 OZ (75 G) BROWN SUGAR
4 OZ (100 G) RAISINS

Topping

2 OZ (50 G) FLOUR
2 OZ (50 G) BUTTER
2 OZ (50 G) GROUND
   ALMONDS
4 OZ (100 G) BROWN SUGAR
1 TSP CINNAMON

Prepare a well-greased 8½ in (21 cm) spring-clip tin.

Cream together the butter and sugar, and beat in the eggs. Fold in the sifted flour and 1 tbsp water and spread this mixture in the cake tin. Peel, core and slice the apples, sprinkle with the lemon juice and toss with the rind, sugar and raisins. Arrange this on top of the cake mixture. To prepare the topping, rub together the flour and butter and then mix in the remaining ingredients. Sprinkle over the apple mixture and bake at 350°F (180°C, Mark 4) for 1¼ hours.

Danish Apple Cake
(AEBLEKAGE)

4½ OZ (115 G) MARGARINE
7 OZ (200 G) CASTER SUGAR
2 EGGS
7 OZ (200 G) PLAIN FLOUR
1½ TSP BAKING POWDER

4 FL OZ (100 ML) MILK
3 DESSERT APPLES
CINNAMON
SUGAR

Set the oven to 350°F (180°C, Mark 4) and grease an 8½ in (21 cm) spring-clip or loose-bottomed cake tin. Cream together the margarine and sugar until light and gradually beat in the eggs. Sift together the flour and baking powder and fold into the mixture with the milk. Peel, core and finely slice the apples. Turn half the cake mixture into the prepared tin and cover with half the apples. Add the remaining mixture and arrange the rest of the apple slices on top. Sprinkle with cinnamon and sugar and bake for 55 minutes.

Apple Macaroon Buns

2 OZ (50 G) BUTTER
2 OZ (50 G) CASTER SUGAR
A FEW DROPS OF VANILLA
  ESSENCE
2 EGG YOLKS
4½ OZ (115 G) SELF-RAISING
  FLOUR
PINCH OF SALT
3 TBSP EVAPORATED MILK
1 LARGE DESSERT APPLE

Macaroon

2 EGG WHITES
3 OZ (75 G) DESICCATED
  COCONUT
3 OZ (75 G) CASTER SUGAR
1 OZ (25 G) PLAIN FLOUR
VANILLA ESSENCE

Cream together the butter, sugar, vanilla essence and egg yolks. Sift together the flour and salt and fold in, along with the evaporated milk. Mix to a firm dough. Chop the apple finely and incorporate it in the dough.

To make the macaroon, whisk the egg whites until stiff and then fold in the remaining ingredients. Grease some bun tins well or set out about sixteen paper cases on a baking tray. Half fill them with the apple mixture, then make a hollow in each with a teaspoon and fill this with a heaped teaspoonful of macaroon mixture. Bake at 350°F (180°C, Mark 4) on a low shelf in the oven for 35 minutes.

Dutch Apple Tea-bread

(APPELBROOD)

4 OZ (100 G) MARGARINE	½ TSP SALT
8 OZ (225 G) SUGAR	3 FL OZ (75 ML) ORANGE
2 EGGS	JUICE
I TSP VANILLA ESSENCE	8 OZ (225 G) COOKING
8 OZ (225 G) PLAIN FLOUR	APPLES, DICED
I TSP BICARBONATE OF SODA	

Set the oven to 350°F (180°C, Mark 4). Cream together the margarine and sugar till light, then beat in the eggs and vanilla essence. Sift together the dry ingredients and fold into the mixture along with the orange juice. Lastly, fold in the apples and turn the mixture into a well-greased 1½ lb (700 g) loaf tin. Bake for 55 minutes.

This is very good spread with whipped cream cheese.

Parisian Gingerbread

8 OZ (225 G) UNSWEETENED APPLE PURÉE (p. 43)	I TSP GROUND GINGER
4 OZ (100 G) DARK BROWN SUGAR	2 OZ (50 G) RAISINS OR CANDIED PEEL
5 OZ (150 G) GOLDEN SYRUP	I TSP CARAWAY SEEDS
3 OZ (75 G) BUTTER	I EGG
8 OZ (225 G) SELF-RAISING FLOUR	I TBSP BRANDY

Make the apple purée and set it aside to cool. Melt the sugar, syrup and butter in a pan, and leave to cool. Sift the flour with the ginger, stir in the raisins or peel and the caraway seeds. Beat the egg with the brandy and add to the flour along with the cooled apple purée and the syrup mixture. Beat well till smooth and pour into a greased 1½ lb (700 g) loaf tin. Bake for 1 hour at 325°F (170°C, Mark 3). After removing from the oven, let the gingerbread cool in the tin for 30 minutes before turning out.

Apple,
Cheese and Walnut Loaf

8 OZ (225 G) WHOLEMEAL FLOUR	4 OZ (100 G) CHEDDAR CHEESE, GRATED
1 TSP BAKING POWDER	2 OZ (50 G) WALNUTS, CHOPPED
1 TSP BICARBONATE OF SODA	
1 TSP CINNAMON	2 APPLES, DICED
½ TSP SALT	3 EGGS, BEATEN
4 OZ (100 G) SUGAR	3 OZ (75 G) BUTTER, MELTED
	1 TBSP MILK

Grease a 1½ lb (700 g) loaf tin.

Sift the first five ingredients into a bowl, stirring in any bran which remains in the sieve. Add the sugar, cheese, walnuts and apples and mix well. Beat in the eggs, one at a time, mixing well after each, then pour in the butter and milk and blend thoroughly. Turn the mixture into the loaf tin and bake at 350°F (180°C, Mark 4) for 1 hour.

Apple Buttermilk Cake

4 OZ (100 G) BUTTER OR MARGARINE	1 EGG
3 OZ (75 G) SUGAR	½ PT (275 ML) BUTTERMILK OR SOUR MILK

I TSP SALT
2 DESSERT APPLES, CORED
 AND SLICED
4 OZ (100 G) PLAIN FLOUR
4 OZ (100 G) WHOLEWHEAT
 FLOUR

I TSP BICARBONATE OF SODA
I TSP CINNAMON

Topping

I TBSP SUGAR
½ TSP CINNAMON

Prepare two well-greased and lined 7 in (18 cm) cake tins.

Cream together the butter and sugar, and beat in the egg. Stir in the buttermilk, salt and apple slices. Sift together the remaining cake ingredients and fold in, adding any bran which remains in the sieve. Pour the mixture into the cake tins, spread it level and sprinkle the topping ingredients over one cake.

Bake at 400°F (200°C, Mark 6) for 10 minutes, and then lower the heat to 350°F (180°C, Mark 4) and bake for a further 30 minutes. When cool, sandwich the cakes together with jam or buttercream.

American Apple and Walnut Cake

You will need an electric mixer or food processor for this recipe.

2 EGGS
I TSP VANILLA ESSENCE
8 FL OZ (225 ML) OLIVE OR
 GROUNDNUT OIL
12 OZ (350 G) SUGAR
8 OZ (225 G) PLAIN FLOUR
I TSP BICARBONATE OF SODA

I TSP SALT
I TSP MIXED SPICE
I LB (450 G) COOKING APPLES
2 OZ (50 G) WALNUTS,
 CHOPPED
2 OZ (50 G) RAISINS

Prepare a well-greased 8 in (20 cm) kugelhopf mould.

Beat the eggs and vanilla essence together till thick and light, then gradually add the oil, beating all the time at high speed. When the mixture is really thick, gradually add the sugar.

Sift together the dry ingredients and fold them in. Add 2 tbsp tepid water to soften the consistency. Peel, core and grate or finely chop the apples, and add to the mixture with the walnuts and raisins.

Spoon into the prepared mould and bake at 350°F (180°C, Mark 4) for 65–75 minutes. Cool in the tin for 15 minutes before turning out.

Apple Plait

Dough

1 LB (450 G) PLAIN FLOUR
½ TSP SALT
1 OZ (25 G) FRESH YEAST
3 OZ (75 G) SUGAR
3 OZ (75 G) BUTTER
¼ PT (150 ML) WARM MILK
1 EGG, BEATEN

Filling

1 OZ (25 G) BUTTER
2 OZ (50 G) BROWN SUGAR
2 OZ (50 G) RAISINS
1 TSP CINNAMON
1 DESSERT APPLE
A LITTLE MILK

Glaze

3 TBSP ICING SUGAR
½ TSP ROSEWATER

Sift the flour and salt into a bowl. Cream the yeast with the sugar, add the butter and beat till smooth. Mix the milk and egg and add. Make a well in the flour, pour in the mixture and beat with a wooden spoon. When the dough becomes firm, knead it with your hands until it is smooth and leaves the sides of the bowl clean. Transfer it to a greased bowl, cover it with clingfilm and leave in a warm place for about an hour. The dough should be doubled in size. Knead it again, turn it over, cover and leave it for a second rising, this time for 30 minutes.

Meanwhile, prepare the filling. Cream the butter and sugar together and add the raisins and cinnamon. Grate the unpeeled apple and quickly mix it in. Now turn the dough on to a floured board and roll it out to an oblong about 12 × 16 in (30 × 40 cm). Cut it lengthways into three equal strips. Spoon a line of filling mixture down the middle of each strip, brush the edges with milk and roll up the dough, pressing the edges and ends firmly together. Press the three ends together and plait. Place the loaf on a greased baking sheet, cover again and prove (leave to rise) for 20 minutes. Set the oven to 400°F (200°C, Mark 6). Bake for about 30 minutes but test with a skewer to check that it is thoroughly cooked. For the glaze, beat the icing sugar and rosewater with 2 tbsp water until smooth and brush the plait with it while still warm.

This is delicious served warm with plenty of butter or curd cheese.

Yugoslav Apple Cake

(POVETICA)

This recipe comes from Istria in the north of Yugoslavia and is similar in concept to a strudel. For a traditional finish, some olive leaves are stuck into the dough prior to baking.

Dough

See previous recipe.

Filling

2 LB (1 KG) DESSERT APPLES
8 OZ (225 G) WALNUTS
4 OZ (100 G) CASTER SUGAR

1 TSP CINNAMON
1 TBSP BRANDY
1 OZ (25 G) BREADCRUMBS
1 EGG, BEATEN
A LITTLE EXTRA CASTER
SUGAR

First make the dough, following the instructions in the recipe for Apple Plait. While it is rising for the second time, prepare the filling. Peel, core and grate the apples and chop the walnuts finely. Mix all the filling ingredients together.

When the dough is ready, turn it on to a floured board and roll it out to an oblong sheet about 14 × 18 in (35 × 45 cm). Spread the filling evenly over it, leaving a small margin round the edges, and roll it up evenly. Press the edges firmly together and lay the cake on a greased baking sheet, curling it into a crescent shape. Glaze it with beaten egg, let it stand for 20 minutes and then bake at 400°F (200°C, Mark 6) for 30 minutes. Sprinkle the warm cake with caster sugar.

Stay me with flagons, comfort me with apples.
Song of Solomon

Penticton
Apple Chiffon Cake

6 EGGS
½ TSP CREAM OF TARTAR
6 OZ (175 G) GRANULATED
SUGAR
5 OZ (150 G) PLAIN FLOUR
3 TSP BAKING POWDER
I TSP SALT

I TSP CINNAMON
4 OZ (100 G) BROWN SUGAR
4 FL OZ (115 ML) VEGETABLE
OIL
I LB (450 G) APPLE PURÉE
(p. 43)

Separate the eggs and beat the whites with the cream of tartar till stiff. Gradually add the granulated sugar and continue beating until the meringue mixture is very stiff and shiny. Sift together the flour, baking powder, salt and cinnamon. Blend into this the brown sugar, and then the egg yolks and the remaining ingredients. Beat till smooth. Fold in the meringue mixture and turn into an ungreased 8 in (20 cm) kugelhopf mould. Bake at 350°F (180°C, Mark 4) for 55–65 minutes. Invert, and cool in the mould. When the cake is cool, loosen the edges and ease it out of the mould.

Apple Crumble Cake
(APFELSTREUSELKUCHEN)

I LB (450 G) TWICE-RISEN DOUGH (see Apple Plait, p. 184)
3–4 FIRM DESSERT APPLES
I OZ (25 G) PLAIN FLOUR
I TSP CINNAMON
2 OZ (50 G) BUTTER
4 OZ (100 G) BROWN SUGAR

Grease a 9 × 13 in (23 × 33 cm) swiss-roll tin and press the dough evenly into it. Peel, core and slice the apples and arrange them in rows on the dough. Rub together the flour, cinnamon and butter, mix in

the sugar and sprinkle this crumble mixture over the apples. Cover the cake and leave it to prove for 30 minutes, meanwhile heating the oven to 375°F (190°C, Mark 5). Bake the cake for 40 minutes.

Cider Apple Sponge

3 EGGS
6 OZ (175 G) CASTER SUGAR
2–3 APPLES
6 OZ (175 G) SELF-RAISING
   FLOUR

PINCH OF SALT
4 OZ (100 G) MELTED BUTTER
I TBSP CIDER
JAM OR CREAM

Set the oven to 350°F (180°C, Mark 4). Grease two 7 in (18 cm) sandwich tins and line the base of each with a circle of greaseproof paper. Grease the papers and dust with caster sugar.

187

Place the eggs and sugar in a bowl and stand it over a saucepan of barely simmering water. Whisk together for about 10 minutes. (This can also be done in an electric mixer, in which case the hot water is not necessary and it will take about 5 minutes.) Peel, core and chop the apples. Sift together the flour and salt over the surface of the mixture and fold in. Then fold in the melted butter, the cider and the apples. Bake for 30–35 minutes. Turn out the cakes and, when cold, sandwich them together with jam or cream or both.

Apple
Upside-down Gingerbread

Topping

2 OZ (50 G) BUTTER
2 OZ (50 G) BROWN SUGAR
I COOKING APPLE

Cake

3 OZ (75 G) BUTTER
6 OZ (175 G) GRANULATED
   SUGAR

I EGG
2 TBSP TREACLE
8 OZ (225 G) WHOLEWHEAT
   FLOUR
I TSP BAKING POWDER
½ TSP BICARBONATE OF
   SODA
I TSP GROUND GINGER
2 COOKING APPLES

Grease and line a deep, 7½ in (19 cm) cake tin.

First prepare the topping. Cream together the butter and brown sugar and spread over the base of the tin. Peel and core the apple, slice it into rings and arrange in the creamed mixture. (You may have to cut some to fit the spaces.)

Cream the rest of the butter with the sugar, and beat in the egg and the treacle. Sift the dry ingredients and fold in gradually, adding any bran that remains in the sieve. Peel, core and dice the remaining apples and fold in, together with enough water (3–4 tbsp) to give a soft consistency. Spoon this mixture over the apple rings and bake at 350°F (180°C, Mark 4) for 60–65 minutes.

Oliebollen

These are traditional New Year's Eve fare in Holland and are often sold at fairs. They are very good hot or cold.

½ OZ (10 G) FRESH YEAST	12 OZ (350 G) PLAIN FLOUR
2 TBSP SUGAR	1 COOKING APPLE
1 EGG	4 OZ (100 G) RAISINS
¼ PT (150 ML) WARM MILK	1 OZ (25 G) CANDIED PEEL
½ TSP VANILLA ESSENCE	OIL FOR FRYING
PINCH OF SALT	ICING SUGAR

Cream the yeast with the sugar, and add 2 fl oz (50 ml) warm water. Beat in the egg, milk, vanilla and salt. Make a well in the flour and pour in the mixture. Work it well with a wooden spoon and then with your hands until it is smooth and elastic. Peel, core and finely chop the apple, and work it in along with the raisins and candied peel. Cover the bowl with clingfilm and leave in a warm place for 1–1½ hours or until the dough has risen to double its size. Heat the oil in a deep pan and drop heaped teaspoonfuls of mixture into it. Turn them if necessary – they may turn themselves while cooking. Lift them out with a slotted spoon on to kitchen paper. Sprinkle with icing sugar.

Danish Apple Ring

Pastry

1 OZ (25 G) FRESH YEAST (OR
  ½ OZ (10 G) DRIED YEAST)
1 TBSP SUGAR
4 TBSP WARM MILK
1 EGG
10 OZ (275 G) STRONG PLAIN
  FLOUR
PINCH OF SALT
8 OZ (225 G) CHILLED BUTTER

Filling

1 LB (450 G) APPLES
1 TBSP APRICOT JAM
GRATED RIND OF 1 LEMON

Glaze

2 TBSP APRICOT JAM
1 OZ (25 G) FLAKED ALMONDS

Cream the yeast with the sugar and gradually add the milk. (If using dried yeast leave for 10 minutes till it becomes frothy.) Beat in the egg. Sift together the flour and salt. Make a well in the centre and pour in the yeast mixture. Work it into the flour and knead till smooth. This should take about 10 minutes. Then wrap it in foil or clingfilm and rest in the fridge for 30 minutes.

Turn it on to a floured surface and roll out to a rectangle. Divide the butter into four portions and dot the surface of the dough with one. Fold the dough in three and roll out again. Repeat this process and then rest the dough in the fridge for 10 minutes. Repeat the process twice more.

Peel, core and grate the apples and mix with the lemon rind and apricot jam. Roll out the dough into a long thin rectangle and spread with the filling. Now roll up the dough like a strudel, lift it on to a baking sheet and curl it round to form a ring. Carefully press the ends together. Make a few cuts across the pastry on top of the ring and bake at 400°F (200°C, Mark 6) for 30 minutes. Remove from the oven, brush with the warmed apricot jam, sprinkle with flaked almonds and return to the oven for a further 10 minutes.

Swabian Apple Cake

Base	Topping
½ OZ (10 G) FRESH YEAST	1½ LB (700 G) DESSERT
8 FL OZ (225 ML) WARM MILK	APPLES
3 OZ (75 G) MARGARINE	2 TBSP CORNFLOUR
3 OZ (75 G) CASTER SUGAR	4 OZ (100 G) SUGAR
VANILLA ESSENCE	1 EGG
PINCH OF SALT	½ PT (275 ML) MILK
1 EGG	8 OZ (225 G) CURD CHEESE
11 OZ (300 G) PLAIN FLOUR	1 TSP RUM FLAVOURING
3 TSP BAKING POWDER	

Stir the yeast into the warm milk. Cream the margarine and sugar together till fluffy, add the vanilla essence, salt and egg and blend well. Sift the flour with the baking powder and add to the mixture alternately with the yeast and milk. Work until smooth. Set the oven to 375°F (190°C, Mark 5).

Spread the mixture in a well-greased 13 × 9 in (33 × 23 cm) swiss-roll tin. Peel, core and slice the apples and arrange them in overlapping rows on the dough.

For the topping, put the cornflour, sugar and egg yolk in a pan; gradually blend in the milk and heat, stirring constantly, until it comes to the boil. Whisk the egg white until stiff and fold into the hot mixture. Work the curd cheese with a wooden spoon or in a food processor till smooth, and add the rum flavouring. Gradually stir into the cornflour mixture. Spread this topping evenly over the apples. Bake for 30–40 minutes.

Devonshire Apple Cake

This close-textured cake is similar to the American apple-sauce cake, but much plainer.

I LB (450 G) UNSWEETENED APPLE PURÉE (p. 43)	4 OZ (100 G) BREADCRUMBS
	I TSP CINNAMON
4 OZ (100 G) BROWN SUGAR	2 OZ (50 G) RAISINS
4 OZ (100 G) BUTTER	I ½ OZ (40 G) CORNFLOUR
2 EGGS	CASTER SUGAR

Grease an 8 in (20 cm) deep cake tin.

Stir the sugar into the warm purée. Beat in the butter, egg yolks, breadcrumbs, cinnamon and raisins. Whisk the egg whites till stiff, sift the cornflour over them and fold it in with a metal spoon. Fold this into the cake mixture. Pour it into the prepared cake tin and bake at 350°F (180°C, Mark 4) for 55 minutes. When cool, sprinkle the cake with caster sugar.

The apple never falls far from the tree.

The rotten apple injures its neighbour.

Proverbs

Toffee Apples

These have been sold at fairs since medieval times. The toffee was made from honey and beeswax until the arrival of sugar from the West Indies.

8 FIRM DESSERT APPLES
8 OZ (225 G) SUGAR
2 TBSP SYRUP
I TSP VINEGAR
8 WOODEN STICKS

Wash and dry the apples. Remove the stalks and push a stick into the centre of each one to reach about half-way down. Put the sugar, syrup and vinegar with 3 tbsp water in a heavy-bottomed pan and stir over a gentle heat till the sugar dissolves. Bring to the boil and cook until the syrup reaches 300°F (150°C) or until a teaspoonful dropped into cold water separates into hard, brittle threads. Remove from the heat.

Dip each apple in the toffee, turning to coat it evenly. Stand the toffee apples on an oiled tray or on non-stick baking paper till they cool and harden. Wrap them in cellophane or clingfilm.

Apple Paste

This recipe can also be made with quinces, or with a mixture of the two fruits.

I LB (450 G) APPLES
8–12 OZ (225–350 G) SUGAR (see recipe)
PINCH OF CINNAMON
PINCH OF GROUND CLOVES
PINCH OF NUTMEG
I TBSP LEMON JUICE

Peel, core and slice the apples. Put them in a pan with 2 tbsp water and cook very gently for about 10 minutes or until soft. Liquidize the cooked fruit till very smooth, or sieve it, and weigh the resulting purée. Put the purée in a heavy-bottomed pan with its exact weight in sugar. Add the spices and lemon juice, blend thoroughly and cook over a gentle heat for about 45 minutes, stirring frequently until the purée becomes thick and translucent and leaves the sides of the pan.

Oil an 8 in (20 cm) square cake tin and sprinkle some sugar over the base. Pour in the apple paste and sprinkle more sugar on top. Let it cool, then leave it in a warm place, e.g. an airing cupboard, for several hours, preferably overnight. When it is very firm, cut into squares or lozenges and store in an airtight tin.

Pippin Knots

Hannah Glasse gives a recipe for an apple paste made with pippins. To make pippin knots, cut the finished paste into narrow strips and form into knots or pretzel shapes. Dust with icing sugar. They can be coloured with red or green food colouring.

> **I heard a sound as of scraping tripe,**
> **And putting apples, wondrous ripe,**
> **Into a cider-press's gripe.**
> Browning, 'The Pied Piper of Hamelin'

13
Preserves

While he from forth the closet brought a heap
Of candied apple, quince and plum and gourd;
With jellies smoother than the creamy curd,
And lucent syrops, tinct with cinnamon;

JOHN KEATS,
The Eve of St Agnes

reserving fruit involves a wide variety of skills, ranging from the simple storage of fruit to drying, freezing, bottling, pickling and the making of jams, jellies and chutneys.

The common factor in all these is the practical desire to save waste at a season of glut and to store the surplus fruit in a safe and palatable form. Another consideration is the availability of other ingredients; for example, in wartime, when sugar was rationed, drying proved a useful alternative to bottling. Similarly, jams and chutneys can be a practical medium for using up odds and ends of other fruit and vegetables, such as green tomatoes.

It is in this section that the crab apple comes into its own. This little wild apple is too tart to be of use in other recipes but it is rich in pectin and makes wonderful jelly. Apart from the hedgerow variety, there are many ornamental crab apples which grace gardens with their blossom in May and provide beautiful red or golden fruit in autumn, and a range of jewel-coloured jellies. The Golden Hornet, John Downie and Siberian Crab will respectively yield jellies of pale gold, deep orange and ruby red. They can also be combined with other hedgerow fruits which are low in pectin, such as blackberry or elderberry, giving a jelly which sets readily, or with herbs, to form a delicious accompaniment to a roast, game or cold meat.

To Freeze Apples

Apple slices

Apple slices can be frozen by a very simple process. Have ready a pan of boiling water and a bowl of ice-cold water to which a few drops of lemon juice have been added. Peel, core and slice the apples. Put them in a wire basket or strainer and dip them into the boiling water for a few seconds; then drain them and dip them into the cold water. Drain thoroughly, pack into polythene bags and freeze.

These slices are not suitable for garnishes but are very useful for pie fillings, purées and baking.

Apple purée

Apple purée can be frozen in polythene bags.

Bottled Apple Purée

This is a very useful method of storing apples. If possible, use small sterilizing jars and use up the purée quickly once it has been opened.

Peel, core and slice the apples into a pan, adding about 1 tbsp water per pound (450 g) of fruit. When soft, beat with a wooden spoon and add 2 tbsp sugar per pound (450 g).

For the sugar syrup, allow 4 oz (100 g) sugar per ½ pt (275 ml) water. Dissolve the sugar in the water over a low heat, bring to the boil and simmer for 2 minutes. The syrup is now ready for use.

Pack the purée into clean sterilizing jars up to the shoulders and top up with some syrup. Stand the jars in a roasting tin lined with newspaper. Do not let them touch each other. Put on the rubber rings or metal tops but do not seal the jars. Heat the oven to 300°F (150°C, Mark 2) and process the jars for about 45 minutes. Remove from the oven and clip down the lids or tighten the screw caps. Leave until completely cold. If any seals are imperfect, use the purée as soon as possible.

Dried Apple Rings

This is the oldest form of preservation. The moisture is extracted from the fruit through the effect of warmth and the bacteria are destroyed. Although now largely superseded by freezing, this method is useful for large quantities since it is very simple and inexpensive. No extra ingredients are needed and the drying frames can be easily made by stretching chicken wire and muslin over an old picture frame. The oven must be only moderately warm so that the fruit keeps its flavour and does not shrivel. Any white coating found afterwards on the fruit is not mould, but dried fruit sugar.

Peel and core the apples, which must be perfectly ripe. Slice them into thick rings and put in lightly salted water for about 10 minutes. Heat the oven to the lowest possible setting. Scald the muslin cloths and spread them over the frames. Arrange the apples on them, not touching each other. Turn them frequently at first to achieve even drying. If possible, leave the oven door ajar to get rid of the moisture. Dry them for several hours until they feel completely dry and exude no juice when pierced by a skewer. This can also be done in an airing cupboard or in the open air (but not in direct sunlight).

After drying, spread out the apple rings to cool and dry completely. They can be stored in airtight jars or hanging on strings in a dry atmosphere.

Before cooking, the rings must be soaked for at least 12 hours. Try to utilize the soaking water when cooking them so that no nourishment is lost.

Apple Caramel Jam

Cox's Orange Pippins are ideal for this jam and the following recipe. The apples must be firm enough to stay intact when cooking.

1 WINEGLASS RUM

4 OZ (100 G) RAISINS

4 LB (1.8 KG) FIRM DESSERT APPLES

SUGAR (see recipe)

Put the rum in a pan and bring to the boil, then remove from the heat, tip in the raisins and leave them to soak. Peel and core the apples. Weigh them and put them in a covered bowl. (There is no need to use lemons or acidulated water as they will soon be used.) Take their weight in sugar and add ¼ pt (150 ml) water per pound (450 g). Heat gently, stirring till the sugar is melted, then boil rapidly until the syrup begins to turn a pale golden colour.

Meanwhile, slice the apples finely and add them, with the raisins and rum, to the caramel. It will harden at first, but keep stirring, pushing the apples down to coat them with the syrup. Turn the heat down and let the jam cook for a further 30–40 minutes, then pot and seal. Label when cold.

Vinetum Britannicum:
OR A

TREATISE
OF
CIDER,

And other Wines and Drinks extracted from Fruits Growing in this Kingdom.

With the Method of Propagating all sorts of Vinous FRUIT-TREES.

And a Defcription of the New-Invented INGENIO or MILL, For the more expeditious making of *CIDER*.

And alfo the right way of making METHEGLIN and BIRCH-WINE.

The Third Impreffion, much Enlarged.

To which is added, A Difcourfe teaching the beft way of Improving BEES.

With Copper Plates.

By *J. Worlidge.* Gent.

LONDON,
Printed for *Thomas Dring*, over againft the Inner-Temple- ate in *Fleet-ftreet.* 1691.

Normandy-style Apple Jam
(CONFITURE DE POMMES NORMANDE)

Follow the recipe for Apple Caramel Jam (p. 199), but add the grated rind of 2 oranges and substitute calvados for the rum.

Apple Ginger Jam

༄༅

This old-fashioned preserve is very quick and simple to make. It is delicious with ice-cream or as a tart filling.

3 LEMONS
4 LB (1.8 KG) COOKING APPLES
2 OZ (50 G) ROOT GINGER
4 LB (1.8 KG) SUGAR
4 OZ (100 G) CRYSTALLIZED GINGER (optional)

Finely pare the lemon rind and squeeze out the juice. Peel, core and slice the apples and drop the slices into a preserving pan containing 1½ pt (850 ml) water and the lemon juice. Tie the lemon rind, apple cores, some of the peel and the bruised root ginger into a piece of muslin or cheesecloth and add to the pan. Bring to the boil and then lower the heat and simmer for about ½ hour. The apples will become pulpy but some pieces will remain whole. Remove the muslin and squeeze, to extract as much flavour as possible.

Now add the sugar and chopped crystallized ginger, if used. Stir gently till the sugar dissolves, then let it boil rapidly for about 15 minutes, or until set. Pot and seal.

Crab-apple Jelly

༄༅

4 LB (1.8 KG) CRAB APPLES
SUGAR (see recipe)

Wash the crab apples thoroughly and cut out any bad bits. Put in a preserving pan with water to cover and simmer till the fruit is soft. Mash to extract as much pectin as possible. Strain through a jelly bag or muslin cloth overnight.

Measure the resulting juice, and for each pint (575 ml) add 1 lb (450 g) sugar to the preserving pan. Stir over a gentle heat to dissolve the sugar, and then boil rapidly for about 10 minutes, or until setting point is reached. Pot and seal.

Crab apples combine beautifully with other fruits. Try the same recipe using half the quantity of crab apples to half of quinces, elderberries or blackberries. The high pectin content of the crab apples insures a much firmer set than is possible with blackberries or elderberries alone.

Mint Jelly

As an alternative to mint sauce, this has the advantage of not mingling with the gravy. It is a good recipe for using up early windfalls which are rich in pectin and coincide with the best season for mint. (Unless of course you have superstitions about St Swithin's day!) Otherwise use cooking apples or a yellow variety of crab apple.

4 LB (1.8 KG) APPLES
¼ PT (150 ML) VINEGAR
JUICE OF ½ LEMON
2 LARGE HANDFULS FRESH MINT
GREEN FOOD COLOURING
GRANULATED SUGAR (see recipe)

Wash the apples, cut into quarters and cut away any bad parts, but don't peel or core them. Put them into a large pan with 3½ pt (2 l) water, the vinegar, lemon juice (including any pips which are squeezed out with it) and one bunch of mint. Bring to the boil, cover the pan and simmer for about an hour, or until the apples are soft. Mash them to extract the pectin and pour the pulp into a prepared jelly bag. Leave to strain overnight.

Measure the juice and pour it into a preserving pan. Add 1 lb (450 g) sugar per pint (575 ml) of juice. Dissolve the sugar over a gentle heat and then boil briskly for about 10 minutes; meanwhile finely chop the second bunch of mint. Draw off the heat and test for a set. When ready, skim and stir in a few drops of green colouring and the chopped mint. Stir till the colour is evenly blended. Pot and seal.

You can use other herbs, e.g. sage or rosemary, instead of mint in this recipe. Another good variation is to use 2 lb (1 kg) gooseberries to 2 lb (1 kg) crab apples, but this time omit the green colouring.

Apple
and Orange Jelly
(GELÉE DE POMMES À L'ORANGE)

This jelly is delicious with meat, as a spread or a glaze. The preparation may seem tedious but the flavour justifies all the hard work!

4 LB (1.8 KG) DESSERT APPLES
JUICE OF ½ LEMON
4 ORANGES
GRANULATED SUGAR (see recipe)
1 LB (450 G) CUBE SUGAR

Wash and dry the apples and chop them roughly but do not peel or core them. Put them in a preserving pan and add 2¾ pt (1.6 l) water and the lemon juice. Bring to the boil, cover and cook very gently for about an hour, mashing the apples occasionally to extract the pectin.

Ladle the pan contents into a scalded jelly bag or muslin cloth and hang it over a basin. Leave it to drip overnight.

Next day wash the oranges and wipe them dry. Rub each sugar cube over the orange skin so that it absorbs as much of the zest as possible. Then cut the oranges in half and squeeze out the juice. Measure the apple juice and pour back into the preserving pan. For each pint (575 ml) add 1 lb (450 g) sugar, of which the cube sugar will be 1 lb (450 g). Add the orange juice and stir over a low heat till the sugar has dissolved. Then bring to the boil and cook rapidly for about 20 minutes or until setting point is reached. Skim, pot and seal.

The apples on the other side of the wall are the sweetest.
W. G. Benham, *Proverbs*

Tomato and Apple Cheese

9 LB (4 KG) TOMATOES
1 VANILLA POD
GRATED RIND OF 1 LEMON
2 LB (1 KG) COOKING APPLES
3 LB (1.4 KG) SUGAR

Put the tomatoes through a liquidizer, a few at a time. Pour the resulting purée into a large preserving pan, add the vanilla pod and lemon rind and cook for 15 minutes. Rub through a sieve and reserve the juice. Meanwhile, cut the apples into quarters and cook in 1 pt (575 ml) water till soft. Mash them and pass them through a sieve. Dissolve the sugar in ½ pt (275 ml) water in the preserving pan and heat gently to form a thick syrup. Pour in the tomato juice and sieved apple and blend well. Bring to the boil and cook briskly for about 30 minutes or until a set is obtained. Leave until completely cold; then pot, seal and label.

Apple Curd

As curd does not keep well, it is advisable to make only small quantities at a time. This recipe makes enough for 3 small jars.

1½ LB (700 G) COOKING APPLES
8 OZ (225 G) SUGAR
2 OZ (50 G) BUTTER
GRATED RIND AND JUICE OF 2 LEMONS
4 EGG YOLKS

Peel, core and slice the apples. Put them in a pan with 3 tbsp water, bring to the boil, cover and cook gently for 10–15 minutes. Sieve or liquidize them and put in the top of a double boiler along with the sugar, butter, lemon rind and juice. Stir over gently boiling water till the sugar dissolves; remove from the heat and beat in the yolks. Return to the heat and stir constantly for about 20 minutes or until the mixture has thickened, but do not let it boil. Pot in small clean jars, cover and seal immediately.

Apple Butter

This preserve was invented by Dutch settlers in Pennsylvania in the mid eighteenth century. It is often served at Thanksgiving.

2 LB (1 KG) COOKING APPLES
1¼ PT (700 ML) CIDER
1½ LB (700 G) SUGAR (see recipe)
1 TSP GROUND ALLSPICE
1 TSP CLOVES
1 TSP CINNAMON

Wash the apples well and cut in quarters. Do not peel or core them, but cut out any bad bits. Put them in a preserving pan with the cider and simmer until they are soft. Now rub them through a sieve and measure the pulp. There should be about 2 pts (1.1 l). Return it to the pan, and for each pint add 12 oz (350 g) sugar. Add the spices and stir the mixture over a gentle heat until the sugar has dissolved, and then bring it to the boil, still stirring gently to prevent sticking. Cook until it acquires a creamy texture. Test it by dropping a spoonful on to a plate. When no liquid runs out it is ready. This only takes about 10 minutes – it is not cooked to the temperature for setting jam or jelly. Pour into clean hot jars and cover. Seal and label when cold.

Old Fortune, like sly Farmer Dapple,
Where there's an orchard, flings an apple.
John Clare, 'Rural Life'

NEW FRUIT

RAISINS

4d. 5d. & 6d. per lb.

CURRANTS

3d. 4d. 5d. 6d. per lb.

J. STONE

Calls the attention of his friends and customers to the above new arrival, and urges them to make their purchases promptly, of the finest qualities of FRUIT for

MINCEMEAT,

And CHRISTMAS PUDDINGS, &c.

STONE'S

NEW SEASON'S

TEAS,

FROM

1s. 4d. to 3s. 4d.
PER LB.

JOSEPH STONE,

111 & 115, King's Road & 50 Radnor St.

CHELSEA.

FREDERICK BELL, STEAM PRINTER, 133, KING'S ROAD, CHELSEA.

Traditional Mincemeat

This recipe, as the name implies, once included meat.

2 LB (1 KG) DESSERT APPLES
4 OZ (100 G) DRIED PRUNES
4 OZ (100 G) GREEN GRAPES
2 OZ (50 G) BLANCHED
   ALMONDS
4 OZ (100 G) DRIED FIGS
1 LB (450 G) SULTANAS

1 LB (450 G) RAISINS
1 LB (450 G) BROWN SUGAR
GRATED RIND AND JUICE OF
   2 LEMONS
¼ PT (150 ML) BRANDY
1 TSP MIXED SPICE

Peel, core and finely chop or mince the apples. Stone the prunes, pip the grapes and chop them. Chop the almonds and figs. Then put everything in a large mixing bowl and stir till well blended. Cover and leave for two days, stirring occasionally so that the fruit soaks up the brandy; then pot and seal.

Green Tomato Mincemeat

In this unusual Canadian recipe the mincemeat is boiled to a thick purée. Despite the large quantity of green tomatoes, the resulting flavour is sweet and toffee-like, equally suitable in mince pies or with a hot sponge pudding.

2 LB (1 KG) GREEN TOMATOES
1 LB (450 G) COOKING APPLES
3 LB (1.4 KG) BROWN SUGAR
8 OZ (225 G) SHREDDED SUET
1 LB (450 G) RAISINS
8 OZ (225 G) MIXED PEEL

½ PT (275 ML) VINEGAR
PINCH OF SALT
1 TBSP CINNAMON
1 TBSP GROUND CLOVES
1 TBSP GROUND NUTMEG

Chop the tomatoes, put them in a preserving pan and add 4 pt (2.3 l) water. Boil gently for 1 hour and leave overnight. Next day, drain the tomatoes and add the apples, peeled and chopped, the sugar, suet, raisins, mixed peel, vinegar and salt. Mix well, bring to the boil and cook gently for 2 hours. Stir in the spices. Pour the mixture into hot clean jars, and pot and seal as for jam.

Red Tomato
and Apple Chutney

4 LB (1.8 KG) RED TOMATOES	2 TSP SALT
1 LB (450 G) ONIONS	2 TSP PEPPER
2 LB (1 KG) DESSERT APPLES	1 LB (450 G) BROWN SUGAR
1½ LB (700 G) RAISINS	1½ PT (850 ML) CIDER
1 TBSP GROUND GINGER	VINEGAR

Skin and roughly chop the tomatoes and onions. Peel, core and chop the apples. Put them in a preserving pan and add all the remaining ingredients. Bring to the boil, and then reduce the heat and simmer gently for 1½–2 hours, stirring occasionally. When the chutney is thick, ladle it into hot clean jars and seal. Label when cold.

Apple
and Gooseberry Chutney

2 LB (1 KG) COOKING APPLES	8 OZ (225 G) RAISINS
2 LB (1 KG) ONIONS	2 TBSP RUM
2 LB (1 KG) GOOSEBERRIES	1 TBSP SALT
1 PT (575 ML) DISTILLED	1 TSP WHITE PEPPER
MALT VINEGAR	1 TSP CINNAMON
1 LB (450 G) BROWN SUGAR	PINCH OF GROUND CLOVES

Peel, core and chop the apples. Peel and finely chop the onions. Top and tail the gooseberries. Put all the ingredients in a preserving pan and cook gently till the sugar dissolves. Bring to the boil, and then reduce the heat and simmer, uncovered, for about an hour, or until the chutney is thick and pulpy. Ladle into clean hot jars and seal. Label when cold.

Apple, Peach and Pumpkin Chutney

This German recipe makes a delicious sweet chutney. As fresh peaches are unlikely to be available when pumpkins ripen, you can use tinned peaches. An excellent recipe for a small pumpkin destined for a Hallowe'en mask!

I LB (450 G) COOKING APPLES	I TBSP POWDERED MUSTARD
I LB (450 G) PEACHES	I TSP SALT
I LB (450 G) ONIONS	GRATED RIND AND JUICE OF
I LB (450 G) PUMPKIN	4 LEMONS
I TSP PEPPERCORNS	I LB (450 G) BROWN SUGAR
½ CINNAMON STICK	½ PT (275 ML) VINEGAR
I TSP CORIANDER	

Peel and core the apples. Skin and stone the peaches (or drain tinned ones). Peel the onions. Scoop out the pumpkin flesh. Chop all the fruit into bite-sized pieces and put in a preserving pan. Tie the peppercorns, cinnamon stick and coriander in a piece of muslin or cheesecloth and add to the pan with the remaining ingredients. Bring to the boil and then simmer, stirring frequently, for about 2 hours, or until the chutney is thick and pulpy. Pot and seal.

Where the apple reddens
Never pry
Lest we lose our Edens
Eve and I.
Robert Browning, 'A Woman's Last Word'

Apple
and Mango Chutney

4 LB (1.8 KG) TART APPLES	4 OZ (100 G) CURRANTS
1 LB (450 G) MANGOES	4 OZ (100 G) SULTANAS
8 OZ (225 G) STEM GINGER	8 OZ (225 G) MIXED PEEL
2 CLOVES GARLIC	1 TSP SALT
2 PT (1.1 L) DISTILLED MALT	1 TSP POWDERED MUSTARD
VINEGAR	1 TSP POWDERED GINGER
1 LB (450 G) BROWN SUGAR	1 OZ (25 G) POWDERED
8 OZ (225 G) RAISINS	ALLSPICE

Peel, core and chop the fruit. Chop the stem ginger and crush the garlic. Put the vinegar into a preserving pan, bring to the boil and add all the other ingredients. Cook over a gentle heat for about an hour or until the chutney is thick, stirring occasionally. Ladle into jars, seal and label.

French Apple Chutney

1½ LB (700 G) DESSERT	SMALL PIECE OF ROOT
APPLES	GINGER
JUICE OF 1 LEMON	1 LB (450 G) BROWN SUGAR
1 LB (450 G) ONIONS	1 TBSP SALT
2 RED PEPPERS	3 TSP POWDERED MUSTARD
	6 OZ (175 G) RAISINS

Peel and core the apples; then grate them or shred them finely in a food processor. Sprinkle immediately with the lemon juice and put in a preserving pan. Peel and finely chop the onions. De-seed and chop the peppers. Bruise the ginger to release the flavour. Add to the apples along with the remaining ingredients. Bring to the boil and then turn down the heat and simmer gently for about an hour, or until the chutney is thick and dark in colour. Stir it occasionally with a wooden spoon. Pot and leave till cold; then label and seal.

Apple
and Onion Pickle

A good recipe for early windfalls. The apples must be prepared very
quickly to prevent discolouring.

1 PT (575 ML) CIDER VINEGAR	1 OZ (25 G) DRIED CHILLIS
2 TBSP SALT	3 LB (1.4 KG) ONIONS
8 PEPPERCORNS	3 LB (1.4 KG) SHARP OR SOUR
8 CLOVES	APPLES

Put the vinegar and salt into a pan. Wrap the spices in a piece of
muslin and leave them to soak in the vinegar for about 30 minutes.
Then bring to the boil and simmer gently for 10–15 minutes. Remove
the spices and let it cool slightly. Meanwhile, prepare the onions and
apples. Peel and finely chop the onions. Peel, core and chop the
apples as quickly as possible and blanch them in boiling water for 2
minutes. Drain them, mix with the chopped onion and pack into hot
clean jars. Pour on the spiced vinegar, cool and seal.

Beetroot
and Apple Chutney

2 LB (1 KG) BEETROOT	8 OZ (225 G) RAISINS
3 LB (1.4 KG) COOKING	1 LB (450 G) BROWN SUGAR
APPLES	2 TBSP MUSTARD SEED
1 LB (450 G) ONIONS	4 OZ (100 G) BLANCHED
1¼ PT (700 ML) VINEGAR	ALMONDS

Cook the beetroot for 1 hour in simmering salted water. Skin while
still warm and leave to cool. Peel, core and slice the apples. Peel and
chop the onions. Put them in a preserving pan with the vinegar,
raisins and sugar. Cook together for about 30 minutes or until soft and
pulpy. Chop the beetroot and add to the mixture along with the other

ingredients. Cook for a further 30 minutes; pour into hot clean jars and seal. Label when cold.

Because of the high apple content, this chutney sets like a jam.

Spiced Crab Apples

These go well with cold meat and can be used in Wassail or Lambswool.

2 LB (1 KG) CRAB APPLES	1 CINNAMON STICK
¾ PT (425 ML) DISTILLED	8 CLOVES
MALT VINEGAR	2 TSP WHOLE ALLSPICE
1½ LB (700 G) SUGAR	BERRIES
1 PIECE OF ROOT GINGER	

Wash the crab apples thoroughly and prick with a fork or fine skewer. Put the vinegar in a large heavy saucepan and add the sugar. Bruise the ginger, break the cinnamon stick in 3 or 4 pieces and tie up with the other spices in a piece of muslin. Add this to the pan and heat gently, stirring until the sugar has dissolved. Bring to the boil, add the crab apples and simmer for 5 minutes. Lift out the fruits with a perforated spoon and pack them firmly into clean hot jars. Boil the vinegar hard till reduced almost by half – it should be the consistency of clear honey. Pour it over the fruit and seal.

And finally, some recipes which were very popular in the seventeenth and eighteenth centuries, and appear in many cookery books of the period. As they are extremely tedious to make, they are quoted here purely for interest.

Pickled Codlins

To pickle codlins, make a Brine of Salt-water, strong enough to bear an Egg, into which put half an hundred of the fairest and largest Codlins you can get;

Malus syluestris.
The wilding or Crab tree.

they must be full grown, but not full ripe; let them lie in this Brine nine or ten days, shifting the pickle every other day, then dry them and very carefully scoop out the Core. Take out the Stalk so whole, as that it may fit in again, and you may leave the Eye in, if you do not put your Scoop quite through: fill it, in the room of the Core, with Ginger slic'd thin and cut short a Clove of Garlick and whole Mustard-seed, as much as it will hold. Put in the piece and tie it up tight. Make your Pickle of as much White-wine Vinegar as will cover them, with slic'd Ginger, Cloves of Garlick and whole Mustard-seed. Pour this Pickle boiling-hot upon them every other Day, for a Fortnight or three Weeks. Stone Jars are best for all Sorts of Pickles.

A Collection of above 300 Receipts in Cookery, Physick and Surgery,
by Several Hands, 1714

Pippin Jelly

This was a method of preserving apples, either whole or sliced, in a jelly made from the fruits themselves and their parings. The resulting preserve is pleasantly flavoured, but you can achieve a similar result by submerging poached fruit in crab apple jelly. Sir Kenelm Digby gives several versions in his book, including the following two. If you try either method, allow the jelly to stand for about 30 minutes after setting point is reached to ensure that the apple slices are evenly distributed.

GELLY OF PIPPINS OR JOHN-APPLES

Cut your Apples into quarters (either pared or unpared). Boil them in a sufficient quantity of water till it be very strong of the Apples. Take the clear liquor, and put to it sufficient Sugar to make gelly, and the slices of Apple; so boil them all together, till the slices be enough, and the liquor gelly; or you may boil the slices, in Apple-liquor without Sugar, and make gelly of other liquor, and put the slices into it, when it is gelly, and they must be sufficiently boiled. Either way, you must put at the last some juyce of Limon to it; and Amber and Musk if you will. You may do it with halves or quartered Apples, in deep glasses, with store of gelly about them. To have these clear, take the pieces out of the gelly they are boiled in, with a slice so as you may have all the rags run from them, and then put neat clean pieces into clear gelly.

SWEET MEAT OF APPLES

My Lady Barclay makes her fine Apply-gelly with slices of John-apples. Sometimes she mingles a few Pippins with the Johns to make the Gelly. But she liketh best the John's single, and the colour is paler. You first fill the glass with slices round-wise cut, and then the Gelly is poured in to fill up the cavities. The Gelly must be boiled to a good stiffness. Then when it is ready to take from the fire, you put in some juyce of Limon, and of Orange too, if you like it: but these must not boil; yet it must stand a while upon the fire stewing in good heat, to have the juyces Incorporate and Penetrate well. You must also put in some Ambergreece, which doth exceedingly well in this sweet-meat.

From *The Closet of the Eminently Learned Sir Kenelm Digby*, 1669

To Make a Sweet Smell

Take the Maste of a Sweet Apple tree, being gathered betwixt the two Lady dayes and put to it a quarter of Damask Rose-water and dry it in a dish in an Oven; wet it in drying two or three times with Rose-water, then put to it an ounce of Benjamin, an ounce of Storax Calamintae, these gums being beaten to powder, with a few leaves of Roses, then you may put what cost of smells you will bestow, as much Civet or Ambergreese and beat it all together in a Pomander or a Bracelet.

From *The Queen's Closet Opened*, 1665

It was from out the rind of one apple tasted that the knowledge of good and evil as two twins cleaving together leaped forth into the world.
John Milton, *Areopagitica*

14
Drinks

When roasted crabs hiss in the bowl . . .

SHAKESPEARE,
Love's Labour's Lost

T he juice of crushed apples, in still or carbonated form, is a very popular drink today. Two other drinks are produced commercially from apples: cider and calvados.

Cider is by far the older drink, so much so that the derivation of its name is uncertain. John Worlidge, who wrote the definitive work *Vinetum Britannicum: a Treatise of Cider* in 1678, states, 'The name Scider being British, having some analogy with the Greek word *Sicera*, is also an Argument that it was a Drink amongst the Antient Britains, they wanting names for new things.' Another possible source is the old Hebrew word *shekar*, meaning 'strong drink'. Worlidge implies that the drink was known in Britain prior to the Roman invasion, when new apple varieties were introduced.

The Norman Conquest is an important landmark in cider history – indeed, the French name for the Battle of Hastings is *La Bataille du Pommier Gris* ('the Battle of the Grey Apple Tree'). The Normans introduced cider apples to Britain and so regular production began.

By the mid thirteenth century the monks at Battle Abbey, so near the site of the grey apple tree, were carrying on a profitable trade in cider. The drink increased in popularity and acquired a good medicinal reputation. Worlidge calls it 'the most wholesome drink that is made in Europe for our ordinary use'. Captain Cook used it as a preventative measure against scurvy.

Cider apples are a special class with fibrous flesh and a high tannin content. There are over 300 varieties. Some have very picturesque names, e.g. Foxwhelp, Redstreak, Slack-my-girdle, Oaken Pin, Great Belly, Lady's Finger and Sheep's Nose.

Calvados is a fiery apple brandy distilled from two-to-three-year-old Normandy cider. Produced mainly in the department from which it takes its name, Calvados has been made since the mid sixteenth century and is often used in recipes *à la normande*. It can be drunk post-prandially, as a liqueur or, as the '*trou normand*', half-way through the meal as an appetizer.

Wassail Bowl

See p. 24 for the history of this dish. Instead of apples, you can use crab apples which have been wrapped and stored, or spiced crab apples.

4 SMALL RED APPLES (OR 8
  CRAB APPLES)
1 CINNAMON STICK
1 PIECE GINGER ROOT,
  BRUISED
3 CLOVES

½ TSP NUTMEG
STRIP OF LEMON PEEL
2 PT (1.1 L) BROWN ALE
4 OZ (100 G) BROWN SUGAR
½ PT (275 ML) SWEET SHERRY

Cut a slit round the middle of the apples and bake at 350°F (180°C,
Mark 4) for 20–30 minutes, or until soft. Tie the spices and lemon
peel in a scalded muslin cloth and warm them in ½ pt (275 ml) brown
ale for 10 minutes. Remove the bag and squeeze to extract the
maximum flavour. Stir in the sugar and let it dissolve; then add the
sherry and remaining ale. Let it simmer very gently for 20 minutes.
Pour the wassail into a punch bowl, float the baked apples on top and
serve at once.

Lambswool

Bands of comely damsels, escorted by their sweethearts went from house to
house, bearing huge brown bowls dressed with ribands and rosemary, and
filled with a drink called 'lamb's-wool', composed of sturdy ale, sweetened
with sugar, spiced with nutmeg, and having toasts and crabs floating within it
. . . Such was the vigil of the year 1600.

W. Harrison Ainsworth,
Auriol, or the Elixir of Life

Lambswool is a Somerset version of Wassail. The ingredients are the
same, but when you bake the apples they should be cored and cooked
for 15–20 minutes. Scoop out the flesh, discarding the skin, and mash
the apple to a smooth pulp. Follow the recipe for Wassail Bowl,
above, and when it is ready pour some liquid into the pulp. Blend till
smooth, and then return to the pan and reheat. Serve very hot.

Non-alcoholic Apple Punch

8 OZ (225 G) SUGAR
5 CLOVES
½ STICK CINNAMON
¾ PT (425 ML) STRONG TEA
JUICE OF ½ LEMON

1 PT (575 ML) APPLE JUICE
1 PT (575 ML) ICED WATER
1 SMALL BOTTLE GINGER ALE
SLICED APPLES FOR GARNISH

Put ½ pt (275 ml) water and sugar in a pan and stir over a gentle heat till the sugar dissolves. Add the spices, bring to the boil and simmer for 10 minutes. Remove the spices and add the tea, lemon juice and apple juice. Stir until well blended and then chill. Just before serving, add the iced water and ginger ale. Serve in a punch bowl with slices of apple floating on top.

Home-made Cider

Since no yeast is used in this recipe, the apples *must* be freshly picked and the cider should not be kept for long after opening.

2 LB (1 KG) APPLES
2 LB (1 KG) SUGAR
JUICE OF 2 LEMONS

Wash and roughly chop the apples, cutting out any bad parts. Measure out 12 pt (6.8 l) hot water. Mince or liquidize the apples, adding some of the hot water. Put this pulp in a large plastic bin, add the rest of the water, cover and leave for 10–14 days. Then add the sugar and the lemon juice. Leave for a further two days.

Skim off any mould which may have formed on the surface. Strain the cider through scalded double muslin and pour into clean bottles. Leave for one week before drinking.

Apple Ginger Cup

1½ LB (700 G) SWEET-FLAVOURED APPLES
1 LEMON
1 OZ (25 G) ROOT GINGER
SUGAR (see recipe)
APPLE SLICES FOR DECORATION

Wash and coarsely chop the unpeeled apples and put them in a preserving pan. Finely pare the lemon rind, squeeze the juice and add to the apples with 4 pt (2.3 l) water. Bruise the root ginger and add to the pan. Bring to the boil and simmer until the apples are soft. Mash thoroughly and strain everything through a sieve (but do not rub the apple pulp through). Measure the liquid and return it to the pan. For each pint (575 ml) add 2 oz (50 g) sugar. Let it dissolve over a low heat, then bring to the boil and cook for 5 minutes. Allow to cool and chill thoroughly. Just before serving float the apple slices on top. Other flavourings may be used, e.g. cinnamon stick or fresh mint.

Fresh Apple Float

2 SMALL DESSERT APPLES
2 TBSP LEMON JUICE
2 TBSP CASTER SUGAR
CRUSHED ICE (optional)
VANILLA ICE-CREAM

Peel, core and chop the apples and put them in a liquidizer with 1 pt (575 ml) cold water, lemon juice and sugar. Liquidize till completely

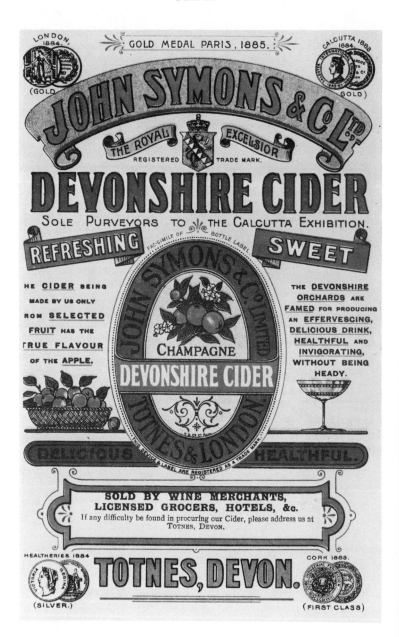

smooth and sieve if necessary. Serve in glasses with crushed ice and float a scoop of vanilla ice-cream on top.

Yoghurt
and Apple Shake

2 TART DESSERT APPLES
¾ PT (425 ML) MILK
¼ PT (150 ML) NATURAL YOGHURT
2 TBSP BROWN SUGAR

Peel, core and chop the apples. Put everything in a liquidizer and blend till completely smooth.

Keep me as the apple of an eye: hide me under the shadow of
Thy wings.
Book of Common Prayer, Psalms

Apples
Powell
Old Wife
Barnett
Wynton Pippin

Scotch Pearmain
Vaughan Pippin
Winch Apple
Spencers Agustina
Nonpareil

Pile Russett
Rushes John
Strip d' Bretagne
Cheradam
St Peters Pippin

FEBRUARY
1732

Greasey Pippin
Pears
Petit St German
Winter Musk
Bergam de Pasq

St Marshall
Lent St German
Winter boon
without Kernell
Dead Mans pears

Double flowering
Petit Boon
Easter Bergamot
Hermaphrodite
Turkey Juniper

Apple Index

EXPLANATION OF TERMS

Seasons		Example
Early	July–first half of Aug.	Beauty of Bath
Second early	second half of Aug.–Sept.	Worcester Pearmain
Mid	Oct.–Nov.	Ellison's Orange
Late	Dec.–Jan.	Crispin
Very late	Feb. onwards	Winston

Russet: brownish spots and roughness on skin of apple, usually a normal characteristic but sometimes due to frost injury.

Sport: a new variety produced by spontaneous mutation from the parent stock, especially in form or colour, e.g. Red Ellison is a sport of Ellison's Orange.

Triploid: a tree which needs two other varieties of the same season to ensure good pollination. Naturally, they themselves are not reliable as pollinators.

Apple Index

Allington Pippin

Origin: King of the Pippins × Cox's Orange Pippin
  Raised in Lincs. by Thomas Laxton, introduced 1896
Season: Mid to late
Skin: Yellow, slight red flush and stripes, thick, tough
Flesh: Crisp, pale yellow
Flavour: Sub-acid, aromatic

Arthur Turner

Origin: Raised at Slough, Bucks., by Charles Turner and named after his
son; introduced 1915
Season: Early to mid
Skin: Yellowish green flushed orange-red with russet, rough
Flesh: Firm, fine, white
Flavour: Acid
Cooker, abundant cropper, long season.

Ashmead's Kernel

Origin: Raised from a pip by Dr Ashmead in Gloucester, probably about
1700
Season: Late to very late
Skin: Green-yellow, brown flush, russeted, dry, moderately tough
Flesh: Firm, yellowish
Flavour: Sweet, aromatic, slightly acid
Keeps very well.

Baker's Delicious

Origin: Found in Wales; introduced 1932 by Bakers of Codsall,
Wolverhampton
Season: Second early
Skin: Yellow flushed orange-scarlet
Flesh: Firm, crisp, creamy white
Flavour: Sweet, aromatic
Good garden variety. Too soft for commercial use.

Beauty of Bath

Origin: First grown at Bailbrook, near Bath. Introduced about 1864 by
Cooling of Bath
Season: Early
Skin: Yellow, flushed red, rough
Flesh: Soft, yellowish, stained red
Flavour: Sweet, strawberry scent
Once our most widely grown dessert variety. Does not keep well. Has a sport,
Crimson Beauty, discovered in 1956.

Belle de Boskoop

Origin: Found at Boskoop, near Gouda, Holland, by K. W. Ottolander in
1856
Season: Very late
Skin: Yellow flushed red, with russet
Flesh: Firm, yellow
Flavour: Acid, aromatic
Triploid. Popular in German and Dutch recipes.

Blenheim Orange

Origin: Raised from a pip by Mr Kempster at Woodstock around 1740
Season: Mid to late
Skin: Yellow streaked red, with russet
Flesh: Crisp, yellow
Flavour: Sub-acid, sweet
Triploid. Will keep till December.

Bramley's Seedling

Origin: Raised from a pip by Mary Ann Brailsford at Southwell between 1809
and 1813; introduced by Merryweather
Season: Late to very late
Skin: Greenish yellow, red flush and stripes
Flesh: Firm, yellowish
Flavour: Acid
Triploid. Most widely grown cooker. Will keep till March. Also a crimson
form known as Crimson Bramley.

Charles Ross

Origin: Peasgood's Nonsuch × Cox's Orange Pippin
Raised by Charles Ross, Welford Park Gardens, Newbury, Berks.;
exhibited 1890
Season: Mid to late
Skin: Pale yellowish green, flushed light red
Flesh: Tender, breaking, tinged orange
Flavour: Sweet tending to sub-acid
Can be baked but also good for dessert. Becomes woolly with keeping.

Chivers Delight

Origin: Raised at Chivers Farm, Histon, Cambs., by Mr Chivers, around
1920
Season: Late
Skin: Green-yellow, orange flush, carmine streaks
Flesh: Firm, yellowish white
Flavour: Sweet, sub-acid, slightly aromatic
Keeps well.

Cox's Orange Pippin

Origin: Raised from a pip, possibly of a Ribston Pippin, by Richard Cox at
Colnbrook, Slough, in 1825; introduced by Charles Turner
Season: Late
Skin: Golden yellow flushed brownish red, russet
Flesh: Tender, crisp, yellow
Flavour: Sweet, slightly sub-acid, aromatic
Very versatile and can be used in almost any recipe. Keeps well.

Crispin (commercial name for Mutsu)

Origin: Golden Delicious × Indo
Raised 1930 at Aomori Apple Experimental Station, Japan; named 1948
Season: Late
Skin: Green to golden with orange flush
Flesh: Firm, coarse, crisp, white
Flavour: Sub-acid, slightly sweet
Triploid. Keeps well.

D'Arcy Spice

Origin: Found in the garden of The Hall, Tolleshunt D'Arcy, Essex, around
1785; introduced by John Harris of Broomfield as Baddow Pippin in 1848
Season: Very late
Skin: Yellowish green flushed dull red, russet patches, tough
Flesh: Firm, fine, crisp, greenish white
Flavour: Sweet, rich, vinous, spicy

Discovery

Origin: Worcester Pearmain × ?Beauty of Bath
Raised by Mr Dummer, Langham, Essex, around 1949; named Discovery in
1962

Season: Early to second early
Skin: Pale greenish yellow flushed bright red with russet
Flesh: Crisp yellowish-white, tinged pink
Flavour: Sub-acid
Excellent pollinator. Does not keep well.

Dunn's Seedling

Origin: Said to have been raised at Kew, Melbourne, Australia; first brought
    to England in 1890
Season: Late to very late
Skin: Pale yellow
Flesh: Crisp, hard, white
Flavour: Sub-acid, sweet

Early Victoria (commercial name of Emneth Early)

Origin: Lord Grosvenor × Keswick Codlin
    Raised by William Lynn, Emneth, Cambs.; first recorded 1899
Season: Early to second early
Skin: Yellowish green
Flesh: Soft greenish white
Flavour: Acid
Excellent cooker but does not keep well.

Egremont Russet

Origin: Unknown; first recorded 1872
Season: Mid
Skin: Yellow, golden-brown flush, nearly covered with russet
Flesh: Compact, firm, cream tinged green
Flavour: Sweet, aromatic, slightly nutty
Will keep until December.

Ellison's Orange

Origin: Cox's Orange Pippin × Calville Blanc
    Raised by Revd C. Ellison, Bracebridge, Lincs. and Mr Wipf, gardener at
    Hartsholme Hall; first recorded 1904, introduced 1911
Season: Mid
Skin: Golden yellow, crimson stripes
Flesh: Tender, yellow
Flavour: Aromatic, sweet, aniseed

Gala

Origin: Kidd's Orange Red × Golden Delicious
  Raised around 1934 by J. H. Kidd in Greytown, Wairarapa, New Zealand
Season: Mid to late
Skin: Yellow, bright orange-red flush, russet, smooth, rather tough
Flesh: Crisp, yellow
Flavour: Sweet, slightly sub-acid
Keeps well but flavour fades with long storage.

George Cave

Origin: Raised 1923 by George Cave at Dovercourt, Essex; named 1945
Season: Early
Skin: Greenish yellow, flushed and striped red, greasy, thick, tough
Flesh: Fine, white, tinged green
Flavour: Sub-acid, sweet, aromatic
Heavy cropper but short keeping life.

Golden Delicious

Origin: Chance seedling found in Clay County, West Virginia around 1899;
  introduced 1914 by Stark Bros.
Season: Late to very late
Skin: Yellow, occasional orange flush
Flesh: Crisp yellowish white
Flavour: Sweet

Golden Noble

Origin: Discovered at Downham, Norfolk and introduced in 1820 by Patrick
  Flanagan, gardener to Sir Thomas Hare, Stowe Hall
Season: Second early to late
Skin: Golden yellow with occasional russet
Flesh: Coarse, firm, crisp, white
Flavour: Acid
Cooker.

Granny Smith

Origin: Chance seed thrown out by Maria Ann Smith, Eastwood, Ryde,
  Paramatta River, New South Wales; already fruiting in 1868
Season: Late to very late
Skin: Green to greenish yellow

Flesh: Hard, crisp, greenish white
Flavour: Sub-acid, moderately sweet
Very versatile. Cooks and keeps well.

Grenadier

Origin: Unknown; first recorded 1862
Season: Early to second early
Skin: Yellowish green, flushed brown, greasy
Flesh: Firm, fine, compact, white tinged green
Flavour: Acid
Cooker. Often sold while still green.

Howgate Wonder

Origin: Blenheim Orange × Newton Wonder
    Raised 1915–16 by G. Wratten, Howgate Lane, Bembridge, Isle of Wight;
    introduced 1932
Season: Late
Skin: Golden yellow with pale red flush and streaks
Flesh: Fairly crisp, cream
Flavour: Sub-acid, sweet
Cooker.

Idared

Origin: Jonathan × Wagenor
  Raised by Leif Verner, Idaho Agricultural Experiment Station, USA;
  introduced 1942
Season: Mid to very late
Skin: Yellow with bright red flush
Flesh: White tinged green
Flavour: Slightly sweet, moderately acid, vinous
Long season, dessert or cooker.

James Grieve

Origin: ?Pott's Seedling × Cox's Orange Pippin
  Raised in Edinburgh by James Grieve; first recorded 1893
Season: Second early to mid
Skin: Pale yellow, flushed and striped red
Flesh: Soft, loose, cream tinged yellow
Flavour: Sweet, sub-acid
Excellent pollinator. Can be used as dessert or cooker.
Short keeping life.

Katy (original name Katya)

Origin: James Grieve × Worcester Pearmain
  Raised 1947 at Balsgård Fruit Breeding Institute, Sweden
Season: Second early
Skin: Yellow flushed scarlet
Flesh: Firm
Flavour: Sweet

Kidd's Orange Red

Origin: Cox's Orange Pippin × Delicious
  Raised 1924 by J. H. Kidd in Greytown, Wairarapa, New Zealand;
  introduced into England in 1932
Season: Late to very late
Skin: Yellow flushed orange-scarlet with red stripes
Flesh: Fine, crisp, firm, cream tinged green
Flavour: Sweet, aromatic, flowery

Lady Sudeley

Origin: Raised 1849 at Petworth, Sussex, by a cottager called Jacob; introduced 1885 by George Bunyard & Co.

Season: Early
Skin: Bright yellow flushed orange red
Flesh: Firm, fine, yellow
Flavour: Slightly sub-acid, sweet

Lane's Prince Albert

Origin: ?Russet Nonpareil × Dumelow's Seedling
    Raised around 1840, either by Thomas Squire of Berkhamsted or by John
    Lane, who introduced it in 1850
Season: Very late
Skin: Yellowish green flushed orange, striped red
Flesh: Very soft, fine, white tinged green
Flavour: Acid
Cooker. Will keep until March.

Laxton's Epicure (also known as Epicure)

Origin: Wealthy × Cox's Orange Pippin
    Raised 1909 by Laxton Bros. Ltd, Bedford; introduced 1929
Season: Second early
Skin: Greenish yellow flushed orange-brown, streaked red
Flesh: Firm, creamy white
Flavour: Sweet, rich, aromatic

Laxton's Fortune (also known as Fortune)

Origin: Cox's Orange Pippin × Wealthy
    Raised 1904 by Laxton Bros. Ltd, Bedford; introduced 1931
Season: Second early
Skin: Pale yellowish green flushed and streaked red
Flesh: Firm, creamy white
Flavour: Sweet, rich, aromatic

Laxton's Superb

Origin: Wyken Pippin × Cox's Orange Pippin
    Raised 1897 by Laxton Bros. Ltd, Bedford; introduced 1922
Season: Late to very late
Skin: Greenish yellow flushed crimson
Flesh: Fine, firm, cream
Flavour: Sweet
Keeps well.

Lord Derby

Origin: Raised around 1850 by Mr Witham, Stockport, Cheshire; first recorded 1862
Season: Mid to late
Skin: Green, turning yellow
Flesh: Firm, pale yellow
Flavour: Sub-acid
Large cooker, sold when green.

Lord Lambourne

Origin: James Grieve × Worcester Pearmain
Raised 1907 by Laxton Bros. Ltd, Bedford; introduced 1923
Season: Mid to late
Skin: Greenish yellow with red flush; becomes greasy when ripe
Flesh: Fine, firm, crisp, cream
Flavour: Moderately sweet, aromatic

McIntosh Red (also known as McIntosh)

Origin: Discovered 1796 by John McIntosh near Dundela, Dundas County, Ontario, Canada; propagated by Allan McIntosh; introduced around 1870.
Season: Mid to late
Skin: Pale yellow, flushed and striped bright red
Flesh: Fine, crisp, tender, white tinged red
Flavour: Sub-acid to sweet, aromatic

Merton Knave

Origin: Laxton's Early Crimson × Epicure
Raised 1948 at Merton, London, by John Innes Horticultural Institution
Season: Second early
Skin: Greenish yellow with extensive flush of bright red
Flesh: Firm, crisp, greenish white tinged yellow
Flavour: Sweet, sub-acid, rich

Merton Worcester

Origin: Cox's Orange Pippin × Worcester Pearmain
Raised 1914 at John Innes Horticultural Institution, Merton, London, by M. B. Crane; named 1947
Season: Second early to mid

Skin: Greenish yellow almost covered bright crimson, russet dots, some
   bloom
Flesh: Fine, firm, crisp, creamy white
Flavour: Sweet, aromatic

Miller's Seedling

Origin: Raised from a pip in 1848 by James Miller at Newbury, Berks.
Season: Second early
Skin: Pale yellow with slight crimson flush
Flesh: Crisp, white, soft
Flavour: Sweet

Monarch

Origin: Peasgood's Nonsuch × Dumelow's Seedling
   Raised 1888, introduced 1918, Seabrook, Chelmsford, Essex
Season: Very late
Skin: Pale yellow, flushed and striped pinkish red, slightly greasy
Flesh: Crisp, loose texture, very tender, very white
Flavour: Sub-acid to sweet
Recommended in Harold Taylor's book *The Apples of England* as a choice
variety for mincemeat.

Newton Wonder

Origin: ?Dumelow's Seedling × Blenheim Orange
   Raised at King's Newton, Melbourne, Derbyshire, by Taylor; introduced
   around 1887
Season: Late to very late
Skin: Bright yellow, scarlet flush and stripes
Flesh: Firm, crisp, yellow
Flavour: Acid
Dessert or cooker. Best as cooker till Christmas, dessert thereafter.

Norfolk Biffin or Beefing

Origin: Unknown; first recorded 1807 in Norfolk
Season: Very late
Skin: Greenish yellow flushed dull crimson
Flesh: Firm, coarse, greenish yellow
Flavour: Sub-acid
Much favoured by Parson Woodforde and Eliza Acton. Best variety for
drying.

Orléans Reinette

Origin: French, otherwise unknown; first described by Knoop in 1776 as 'a magnificent fruit'
Season: Late to very late
Skin: Golden with slight red flush and russet patches
Flesh: Fine, crisp, yellow
Flavour: Sweet, sub-acid, perfumed
Keeps until the New Year.

Peasgood's Nonsuch

Origin: Raised around 1858 from a pip by Mrs Peasgood at Stamford, Lincs.
Season: Second early to mid
Skin: Greenish yellow with carmine flush and stripes
Flesh: Crisp, firm, coarse, yellowish white
Flavour: Sub-acid, aromatic
Can be used as dessert or cooker.

Pomme d'Api

Origin: Thought to have been found in the Forest of Apis, Brittany; recorded 1628
Season: Mid to very late
Skin: Yellow flushed red
Flesh: Tender, white
Flavour: Sweet, aromatic

Queen Cox

Origin: Bud sport of Cox's Orange Pippin, discovered at Appleby Fruit Farm, Kingston Bagpuize, Oxon. Received by National Fruit Trial 1953. Similar in all aspects to the Cox's Orange Pippin but brighter red.

Red Delicious

Origin: Originated 1880 as sprout from rootstock on farm of Jesse Hiatt near Peru, Iowa, USA; introduced 1895 in USA by Stark Bros.; into England around 1912
Season: Late
Skin: Greenish yellow with red flush and stripes
Flesh: Firm, crisp, creamy white
Flavour: Sweet

Red Ellison

Origin: Sport of Ellison's Orange, found 1948 in H. C. Selby's orchard, Walpole St Peter, Wisbech, Cambs. Similar in all aspects to Ellison's Orange except that the fruit is nearly covered with crimson flush.

Revd W. Wilks

Origin: Peasgood's Nonsuch × Ribston Pippin
  Raised by Veitch, Chelsea, recorded 1904, introduced 1908
Season: Mid
Skin: Pale yellow with slight flush and stripes
Flesh: Tender, white
Flavour: Acid
Can be used as cooker or dessert. Keeps for only a few weeks.

Ribston Pippin

Origin: Raised from a pip brought from Rouen and planted at Ribston Hall, Knaresborough, Yorkshire; discovered 1709
Season: Late
Skin: Yellow flushed orange, streaked red, greasy
Flesh: Fine, yellowish
Flavour: Sub-acid, sweet, aromatic
Triploid.

Rosemary Russet

Origin: Unknown; first described 1831
Season: Late to very late
Skin: Yellow, tinged green, flushed brownish red with russet
Flesh: Fine, firm, white tinged yellowish green
Flavour: Sweet, sub-acid, aromatic
Keeps well.

Spartan

Origin: McIntosh Red × Yellow Newtown Pippin
  Raised 1926 at Dominion Experimental Station, Summerland, British Colombia, Canada, by R. C. Palmer; introduced 1936
Season: Mid to very late
Skin: Yellow, almost completely flushed deep purplish red with bloom, thick
Flesh: Firm, crisp, fine, very white
Flavour: Sub-acid
Keeps well.

Starking

Origin: Bud mutation of Delicious; discovered 1921 by Lewis Mood at Monroeville, New Jersey, USA; introduced 1924
Season: Very late
Skin: Yellow, striped and flushed dark red
Flesh: Firm, fine, yellow
Flavour: Sweet

Sturmer Pippin

Origin: ?Ribston Pippin × Nonpareil
Raised by Dillistone at Sturmer, Suffolk; first recorded 1831, now grown mainly in Tasmania
Season: Very late
Skin: Greenish yellow flushed brownish red, smooth
Flesh: Very firm, pale greenish white
Flavour: Acid

Sunset

Origin: Raised from a Cox's Orange Pippin pip in 1918 by G. C. Addy at Ightham, Kent; named 1933
Season: Mid to late
Skin: Deep orange-yellow with orange flush
Flesh: Firm, crisp, fine, tender, creamy yellow
Flavour: Sweet, slightly acid, aromatic
Keeps well.

Tydeman's Early Worcester

Origin: McIntosh Red × Worcester Pearmain
Raised 1929 at East Malling Research Station, Maidstone, Kent, by H. M. Tydeman; introduced 1945
Season: Second early
Skin: Dull yellow covered with deep red flush
Flesh: Crisp, fine, very white
Flavour: Sweet, sub-acid, scented

Tydeman's Late Orange

Origin: Laxton's Superb × Cox's Orange Pippin
Raised 1930 at East Malling Research Station, Maidstone, Kent, by H. M. Tydeman; introduced 1949
Season: Late to very late
Skin: Golden yellow tinged green, orange-red flush

Flesh: Firm, crisp, fine, cream
Flavour: Sweet, sub-acid, aromatic

Tydeman's Michaelmas Red

Origin: McIntosh Red × Worcester Pearmain
    Raised 1929 at East Malling Research Station, Maidstone, Kent, by H. M. Tydeman
Season: Mid to late
Skin: Pale greenish yellow, nearly covered in deep crimson; becomes very dark with keeping
Flesh: Soft, greenish white
Flavour: Sweet, sub-acid

Winston (original name Winter King)

Origin: Cox's Orange Pippin × Worcester Pearmain
    Raised 1920 at Welford, Berks., by William Pope; introduced 1935
Season: Late to very late
Skin: Greenish yellow, orange-red flush with russet
Flesh: Firm, crisp, tender, greenish white
Flavour: Slightly sweet, sub-acid

Worcester Pearmain

Origin: Said to be raised from a Devonshire Quarrenden pip by Mr Hale at Swan Pool near Worcester; introduced 1874 by Smith of Worcester
Season: Second early
Skin: Pale yellow flushed bright red with russet

Flesh: Firm, crisp, white
Flavour: Sweet, perfumed, strawberry flavour
Keeps for only a few weeks.

Reproduced by kind permission of the Director, National Fruit Trials, Ministry of Agriculture, Fisheries and Food.
© Crown Copyright 1987

RECENT VARIETIES

The following are new apple varieties which have been raised at East Malling Research Station, Kent.

Bountiful

Parentage: Derived from an open pollinated seedling from Cox's Orange Pippin
Season: Mid
Skin: Predominantly green with occasional orange-red patches or red stripes
Flesh/flavour: Sweet and delicious – needs very little sugar in cooking
Storage: Keeps until January in cool storage
First new cooker to be introduced for fifty-five years. Can be eaten as a dessert apple in late winter.

Fiesta

Parentage: Cox's Orange Pippin × Idared
Season: Mid
Skin: Bright red flush with stripes on a yellow background
Flesh/flavour: Juicy, similar in flavour to Cox but crisper
Storage: Keeps well until April in cool storage

Greensleeves

Parentage: James Grieve × Golden Delicious
Season: Early
Skin: Green to greenish-yellow with distinct lenticels and a trace of russet round the stalk
Flesh: Crisp, juicy
Flavour: Moderately acid
Storage: Fruit picked in mid-September will keep till late November. Fruit picked later has a shorter shelf-life and should be used as soon as possible

Jester

Parentage: Worcester Pearmain × Starkspur Golden Delicious
Season: Mid
Skin: Bright red on a yellow-green background
Flesh/flavour: Crisp, juicy with a good texture and flavour
Storage: Keeps until December in cool storage

Jupiter

Parentage: Cox's Orange Pippin × Starking
Season: Mid
Skin: Orange-red flush with stripes on a greenish-yellow background
Flesh/flavour: Juicy with good texture and flavour similar to Cox
Storage: Will keep till April
Triploid.

Kent

Parentage: Cox's Orange Pippin × Jonathan
Season: Late
Skin: Red on a green background
Flesh: Creamy white, crisp, juicy
Flavour: Aromatic
Storage: Keeps until March

Redsleeves

Parentage: Exeter Cross × an EMRS seedling, TSR 15T3
Season: Second early
Skin: Predominantly red on a yellow-green background
Flesh: Crisp, juicy
Flavour: Sweet
Storage: Retains flavour and texture for at least a month when stored at room temperature
Scab and mildew resistant.

Suntan

Parentage: Cox's Orange Pippin × Court Pendu Plat
Season: Late
Skin: Orange-red flush with darker stripes on a green ground, becomes golden yellow as fruit ripens
Flesh: Yellow, crisp
Flavour: Very sharp till fruit is fully ripe when the aromatic flavour is most marked; to achieve full flavour, the fruit should be eaten when the ground colour turns from green to yellow; unlike many varieties, the flesh remains crisp and juicy
Storage: If picked before the first week of October, the aromatic flavour will not develop fully. Suntan should not be stored beyond the end of January
Triploid.

Nursery Gardens

The following nursery gardens stock large selections of apple trees including many unusual varieties. Catalogues are available from most of them and some will dispatch orders by post. This information is up to date at the time of publication.

BERKSHIRE

J. C. Allgrove, The Nursery, Middle Green, Langley, Slough, Berks s L3 6B U
Tel. 0753 20155
230 varieties

BUCKINGHAMSHIRE

Buckingham Nurseries and Garden Centre, Tingewick Road, Buckingham M K18 1ST
Tel. 0280 813556
22 varieties

CHESHIRE

Bridgemere Nurseries Ltd, Bridgemere, nr Nantwich, Cheshire
Tel. 09365 239
30 varieties

DEVONSHIRE

St Bridget Nurseries Ltd, Old Rydon Lane, Exeter, Devon E X2 7J Y
Tel. 039287 3672
23 varieties

DORSET

Dayspring Nursery, Quarr, Buckhorn Weston, Gillingham, Dorset s P8 5P A
Tel. 074 76 3030
65 varieties and grafting to order

C. W. Groves & Son, West Bay Road, Bridport, Dorset D T6 4B A
Tel. 0308 22654
20 varieties

GLOUCESTERSHIRE

Highfield Nurseries, Whitminster, Glos GL2 7PL
Tel. 0452 740266
32 varieties

HAMPSHIRE

Blackmoor Fruit Nurseries, Blackmoor, Liss, Hants GU22 6BS
Tel. 04203 3576
56 varieties and farm shop

Family Trees, Summerlands, Curdridge, Botley, Southampton, Hants
SO3 2HB
Tel. 04892 6680
65 varieties

Hillier Nurseries (Winchester) Ltd, Ampfield House, Ampfield, nr Romsey,
Hants SO5 9PA
Tel. 0794 68733
20 varieties

ISLE OF WIGHT

Deacons Nursery, Godshill, Isle of Wight PO38 3HW
Tel. 0983 840750
186 varieties

KENT

New Tree Nurseries (P. H. Harding), 2 Nunnery Road, Canterbury, Kent
CT1 3LS
Tel. 0227 61209
Almost any variety can be grafted to order

Keepers Nursery, 446 Wateringbury Road, East Malling, Maidstone, Kent
ME19 6JJ
Tel. 0622 813008
140 varieties

Romney Marsh Garden Centre (Kennington Garden Nursery), Hamstreet,
Ashford, Kent TN26 2QP
Tel. 023 373 2613
44 varieties

LINCOLNSHIRE

Eden Nurseries, Old Bolingbroke, Spilsby, Lincs
Tel. 07903 582
50 varieties and stock being increased each year

NORFOLK

Whispering Tree Nursery, Wimbotsham, Norfolk PE34 8QB
Tel. 0366 388752
69 varieties in stock, but many more available for budding to order

SOMERSET

Scotts Nurseries (Merriott) Ltd, Merriott, Somerset TA16 5PL
Tel. 0460 72306
170 varieties

Tatworth Fruit Farm Garden Centre, Tatworth, Chard, Somerset TA20 2SG
Tel. 0460 20272
35 varieties and farm shop

SUFFOLK

F. G. Barcock & Co., Garden House Farm, Drinkstone, Bury St Edmunds,
Suffolk IP30 9TN
Tel. 04493 249
45 varieties; orders not available by post

SUSSEX

T. A. Redman, Elms Farm, Ancton Lane, Middleton-on-Sea, Bognor
Regis, W. Sussex PO22 6NJ
Tel. 024369 4447
38 varieties

YORKSHIRE

R. V. Roger Ltd, The Nurseries, Pickering, N. Yorkshire YO18 7HG
Tel. 0751 72226
42 varieties

Pick Your Own and Farm Shops

These farm shops have large selections of apple varieties. Availability varies according to season (see Explanation of Terms, p. 227) and not all varieties will be in stock at the same time. If in doubt it is worth telephoning in advance to check which apples are available. This information is up to date at the time of publication.

BERKSHIRE
Bowdenside Farm, Yattendon Road, Pangbourne, Berks RG8 8PT
Tel. 07357 4152
12 varieties and home-pressed apple juice

BUCKINGHAMSHIRE
Home Cottage Farm, Bangors Road South, Iver Heath, Bucks SL0 0BB
Tel. 0753 653064
12 varieties

CAMBRIDGESHIRE
Elbourn Apples, 25 Whitecroft Road, Meldreth, Cambs
Tel. 0763 60332
16 varieties

CHESHIRE
L. Haworth & Son at Haworth's Fruit Farm, Edisbury Fruit Farm, Yeld Lane, Kelsall, Cheshire CW6 0TE
Tel. 0829 51300/51188
14 varieties

DORSET
Elwell Fruit Farm, Netherbury, Bridport, Dorset DT6 5LF
Tel. 030888 283
23 varieties

ESSEX
Bradfield Fruit Farm, The Street, Bradfield, nr Manningtree, Essex CO11 2UU
Tel. 025587 696
22 varieties

Crapes Fruit Farm, Rectory Road, Aldham, nr Colchester, Essex CO6 3RR
Tel. 0206 210406
Britain's largest fruit farm, stocking about 160 varieties, some very old and rare. Closed Sundays

HAMPSHIRE
Blackmoor Estate Ltd, Blackmoor, Liss, Hants GU22 6BS
Tel. 04203 3576
13 varieties. Annual apple-tasting day in October

KENT
W. Brice & Sons Ltd, Mockbeggar Farm, Higham, Rochester, Kent ME3 8EU
Tel. 0634 717425 (office), 725664 (shop)
12 varieties

Hewitts Farm, Chelsfield, Orpington, Kent BR6 7QR
Tel. 0959 34271/34666
41 varieties. Apple Festival held each year in October with competitions, apple tasting and home-pressed apple juice

NORFOLK
Doubleday Bros., Saddlebow, King's Lynn, Norfolk
Tel. 055 385 206
21 varieties, including the historic Norfolk Biffin, recently introduced

Tyler's, The Cedars, Thorpe Market Road, Roughton, Norwich, Norfolk NR11 8TB
Tel. 026379 777
14 varieties

OXFORDSHIRE
Midwinter Fruit Farm, Milton Hill, Abingdon, Oxon OX14 4DP
Tel. 0235 831247
15 varieties

Millets Farm & Crabtree Pick Your Own, Millets Farm, Garford, Abingdon, Oxon OX13 5PD
Tel. 0865 391266 (Millets Farm), 39155 (Crabtree Farm)
12 varieties

SOMERSET
Charlton Orchards, Creech St Michael, Taunton, Somerset TA3 5PF
Tel. 0823 412959
14+ varieties. New ones are constantly being added

North Perrott Fruit Farm, North Perrott, Crewkerne, Somerset TA18 7SU
Tel. 0460 72883
20 varieties

Stawell Fruit Farm, Stawell, Bridgwater, Somerset
Tel. 0278 722732
20 varieties

Tatworth Fruit Farm, Tatworth, Chard, Somerset TA20 2SG
Tel. 0460 20272
17 varieties

West Bradley Farm, West Bradley, nr Glastonbury, Somerset BA6 8LT
Tel. 04585 0227
18 varieties

SURREY

Avalon Farm, Old Barn Lane, Churt, Farnham, Surrey GU10 2NA
Tel. 042873 5161
12 varieties

SUSSEX

Hunt's Fruit, Sharewood Farm, New England Lane, Sedlescombe, Battle, Sussex
Tel. 042487 354/567
25+ varieties and cider apples

Ringdon Farm Ltd, London Road, Hurst Green, Etchingham, E. Sussex
TN1 7QY
Tel. 058087 385
22 varieties

WARWICKSHIRE

Snitterfield Fruit Farm, Kings Lane, Stratford-upon-Avon, Warwickshire
CV37 0QA
Tel. 0789 731/244 (office), 711 (recorded information)
19 varieties

WORCESTERSHIRE

John Dowty Ltd, Fruit & Vegetable Centre, Ombersley, Droitwich, Worcs
WR9 0JH
Tel. 0905 620404
13 varieties. Imported apples also stocked, therefore apples available all year round. This firm, started in 1921, claims to be the oldest farm shop in Britain

YORKSHIRE

Ampleforth College Orchards, Ampleforth College, Ampleforth, Yorks,
YO6 4HA
Tel. 04393 485
18 varieties, also publication *Cooking Apples*

SCOTLAND

Priorwood Orchard, Melrose, Roxburghshire, Scotland
Tel. 089682 2493/2965 (shop), 2555 (tourist information centre)
Priorwood has a 'Historic Apple Walk' of trees arranged chronologically,
from Roman times to the present day. The apples themselves are not sold,
but the shop has a variety of apple products – jams, jellies, chutneys, etc. –
on sale.

Bibliography

The Form of Cury (1390)
Gervase Markham, The English Huswife (1615)
The Queen's Closet Opened (1656)
Robert May, The Accomplish'd Cook (1665)
Sir Kenelm Digby, The Closet of the Eminently Learned Sir Kenelm Digby (1669)
John Evelyn, A Discourse on Sallets (1669)
John Worlidge, Vinetum Britannicum: a Treatise of Cider (1678)
John Aubrey, Remains of Gentilisme (1686)
John Evelyn, The Compleat Gard'ner (1693)
A Collection of above 300 Receipts in Cookery, Physick and Surgery, by several hands (1714)
Hannah Glasse, The Art of Cookery made Plain and Easy, by a Lady (1747)
Elizabeth Cleland, A New and Easy Method of Cooking (1759)
Hannah Glasse, The Compleat Confectioner (1770)
Susannah McIver, Cookery and Pastry (1773)
John Farley, The London Art of Cookery (1783)
Brillat-Savarin, La Physiologie du Goût (1825)
Meg Dods, Cook and Housewife's Manual (1826)
John Brand, Observations on the Popular Antiquities of Great Britain (1849)
Isabella Beeton, The Book of Household Management (1861)
C. H. Poole, Customs, Superstitions and Legends (1877)
Andrew Tuer, Old London Street Cries (1885)
Celia Fiennes, Through England on a Side Saddle (1888)
William Walsh, Curiosities of Popular Customs (1897)
William Hazlitt, Faiths and Folklore (ed. 1905)
C. A. Miles, Christmas in Ritual and Tradition (1912)
J. Rendel Harris, Origin and Meaning of Apple Cults (1919)
James Woodforde, The Diary of a Country Parson (first published 1924)
A. R. Wright, English Folklore (1928)
Edward Bunyard, The Anatomy of Dessert (1933)
Harold Taylor, The Apples of England (1945)
Muriel Smith, The National Apple Register of the United Kingdom (1971)

Weights and Measures

These equivalents between imperial and metric measurements are convenient approximations.

WEIGHTS		LIQUID MEASURES	
½ oz	10 g	¼ pt	150 ml
1 oz	25 g	½ pt	275 ml
1½ oz	40 g	¾ pt	425 ml
2 oz	50 g	1 pt	575 ml
2½ oz	60 g	1¼ pt	700 ml
3 oz	75 g	1½ pt	850 ml
4 oz	100 g	2 pt	1.1 l
5 oz	150 g	3 pt	1.7 l
6 oz	175 g	3½ pt	2 l
7 oz	200 g	4 pt	2.3 l
8 oz	225 g	6 pt	3.4 l
9 oz	250 g	8 pt	4.5 l
10 oz	275 g	12 pt	6.8 l
11 oz	300 g		
12 oz	350 g	2 pt pudding basin or	
1 lb	450 g	pie dish = 1 l dish	
1½ lb	700 g		
2 lb	1 kg	tsp	5 ml
3 lb	1.4 kg	dessertspoon	10 ml
4 lb	1.8 kg	tbsp	15 ml

MEASUREMENT	
7 in	18 cm
8 in	20 cm
8½ in	21 cm
9 in	23 cm
10 in	25 cm
13 in	33 cm

All the eggs used in these recipes are Size 4.

All spoon measures are level.

Oven Temperatures

Oven Heat	Gas Mark	Fahrenheit	Centigrade
Very cool	¼	225°F	110°C
Very cool	½	250°F	130°C
Cool	1	275°F	140°C
Cool	2	300°F	150°C
Moderate	3	325°F	170°C
Moderate	4	350°F	180°C
Fairly hot	5	375°F	190°C
Hot	6	400°F	200°C
Hot	7	425°F	220°C
Very hot	8	450°F	230°C
Very hot	9	475°F	240°C

Picture Credits

p. 137   Gerard's *Herball* (Geoff Howard)
p. 139   Fruit seller (Fotomas Index)
p. 142   Baking or boiling apples (JJ Collection, Bodleian Library)
p. 154   Pommes cuites au four, Paris, 1739 (Bibliothèque des Arts Decoratifs – J.-L. Charmet)
p. 160   Gathering blackberries, c. 1880 (Mary Evans Picture Library)
p. 166   Creams and jellies from Mrs Beeton, *The Book of Household Management*, revised ed., 1901
p. 171   Marchande de pommes, nineteenth-century engraving (Bibliothèque des Arts Decoratifs – J.-L. Charmet)
p. 172   'A Apple Pie', from *A Apple Pie*, 1886 (Bridgeman Art Library)
p. 187   Apple pressing (courtesy Bulmers)
p. 194   Pajaro Valley apples, label (Robert Opie)
p. 200   *Vinetum Britannicum*, 3rd ed., 1691 (Museum of Cider, Hereford)
p. 206   Mincemeat (JJ Collection, Bodleian Library)
p. 211   Chutney label (JJ Collection, Bodleian Library)
p. 214   Crabapple, from Gerard's *Herball*, 1633 (Royal Horticultural Society – Geoff Howard)
p. 218   Cider glass (courtesy Bulmers)
p. 220   Cider glass (courtesy Bulmers)
p. 223   Apple pressing from *Vinetum Britannicum*, 1678 (BBC Hulton Picture Library)
p. 224   Devonshire cider (JJ Collection, Bodleian Library)
p. 226   Apples and pears (Fotomas Index)
p. 233   Lithograph, 1835 (Bibliothèque des Arts Decoratifs – J.-L. Charmet)
p. 241   Trade card (courtesy Museum of Cider, Hereford)
p. 243   Trade card (courtesy Museum of Cider, Hereford)
p. 247   'Fancy Soccer Brand apples' (Robert Opie)
p. 251   Chutney relish label (Bodleian Library).

General Index

257

Index of Recipes

FOR THE BEST IN PAPERBACKS, LOOK FOR THE

In every corner of the world, on every subject under the sun, Penguin represents quality and variety – the very best in publishing today.

For complete information about books available from Penguin – including Pelicans, Puffins, Peregrines and Penguin Classics – and how to order them, write to us at the appropriate address below. Please note that for copyright reasons the selection of books varies from country to country.

In the United Kingdom: For a complete list of books available from Penguin in the U.K., please write to *Dept E.P., Penguin Books Ltd, Harmondsworth, Middlesex, UB7 0DA*

In the United States: For a complete list of books available from Penguin in the U.S., please write to *Dept BA, Penguin, 299 Murray Hill Parkway, East Rutherford, New Jersey 07073*

In Canada: For a complete list of books available from Penguin in Canada, please write to *Penguin Books Canada Ltd, 2801 John Street, Markham, Ontario L3R 1B4*

In Australia: For a complete list of books available from Penguin in Australia, please write to the *Marketing Department, Penguin Books Australia Ltd, P.O. Box 257, Ringwood, Victoria 3134*

In New Zealand: For a complete list of books available from Penguin in New Zealand, please write to the *Marketing Department, Penguin Books (NZ) Ltd, Private Bag, Takapuna, Auckland 9*

In India: For a complete list of books available from Penguin, please write to *Penguin Overseas Ltd, 706 Eros Apartments, 56 Nehru Place, New Delhi, 110019*

In Holland: For a complete list of books available from Penguin in Holland, please write to *Penguin Books Nederland B.V., Postbus 195, NL-1380AD Weesp, Netherlands*

In Germany: For a complete list of books available from Penguin, please write to *Penguin Books Ltd, Friedrichstrasse 10 – 12, D-6000 Frankfurt Main 1, Federal Republic of Germany*

In Spain: For a complete list of books available from Penguin in Spain, please write to *Longman Penguin España, Calle San Nicolas 15, E-28013 Madrid, Spain*

FOR THE BEST IN PAPERBACKS, LOOK FOR THE

COOKERY IN PENGUINS

Jane Grigson's Vegetable Book   Jane Grigson

The ideal guide to the cooking of everything from artichoke to yams, written with her usual charm and depth of knowledge by 'the most engaging food writer to emerge during the last few years' – *The Times*

More Easy Cooking for One or Two   Louise Davies

This charming book, full of ideas and easy recipes, offers even the novice cook good wholesome food with the minimum of effort.

The Cuisine of the Rose   Mireille Johnston

Classic French cooking from Burgundy and Lyonnais, including the most succulent dishes of meat and fish bathed in pungent sauces of wine and herbs.

Good Food from Your Freezer   Helge Rubinstein and Sheila Bush

Using a freezer saves endless time and trouble and cuts your food bills dramatically; this book will enable you to cook just as well – perhaps even better – with a freezer as without.

An Invitation to Indian Cooking   Madhur Jaffrey

A witty, practical and delightful handbook of Indian cookery by the much loved presenter of the successful television series.

Budget Gourmet   Geraldene Holt

Plan carefully, shop wisely and cook well to produce first-rate food at minimal expense. It's as easy as pie!

FOR THE BEST IN PAPERBACKS, LOOK FOR THE

COOKERY IN PENGUINS

Mediterranean Food   Elizabeth David

Based on a collection of recipes made when the author lived in France, Italy, the Greek Islands and Egypt, this was the first book by Britain's greatest cookery writer.

The Vegetarian Epicure   Anna Thomas

Mouthwatering recipes for soups, breads, vegetable dishes, salads and desserts that any meat-eater or vegetarian will find hard to resist.

A Book of Latin American Cooking   Elisabeth Lambert Ortiz

Anyone who thinks Latin American food offers nothing but *tacos* and *tortillas* will enjoy the subtle marriages of texture and flavour celebrated in this marvellous guide to one of the world's most colourful *cuisines*.

Quick Cook   Beryl Downing

For victims of the twentieth century, this book provides some astonishing gourmet meals – all cooked in under thirty minutes.

Josceline Dimbleby's Book of Puddings, Desserts and Savouries

'Full of the most delicious and novel ideas for every type of pudding' – *Lady*

Chinese Food   Kenneth Lo

A popular step-by-step guide to the whole range of delights offered by Chinese cookery and the fascinating philosophy behind it.

COOKERY IN PENGUINS

The Beginner's Cookery Book   Betty Falk

Revised and updated, this book is for aspiring cooks of all ages who want to make appetizing and interesting meals without too much fuss. With an emphasis on healthy eating, this is the ideal starting point for would-be cooks.

The Pleasure of Vegetables   Elisabeth Ayrton

'Every dish in this beautifully written book seems possible to make and gorgeous to eat' – *Good Housekeeping*

French Provincial Cooking   Elizabeth David

'One could cook for a lifetime on this book alone' – *Observer*

Jane Grigson's Fruit Book

Fruit is colourful, refreshing and life-enhancing; this book shows how it can also be absolutely delicious in meringues or compotes, soups or pies.

A Taste of American Food   Clare Walker

Far from being just a junk food culture, American cuisine is the most diverse in the world. Swedish, Jewish, Creole and countless other kinds of food have been adapted to the new environment; this book gives some of the most delicious recipes.

Leaves from Our Tuscan Kitchen   Janet Ross and Michael Waterfield

A revised and updated version of a great cookery classic, this splendid book contains some of the most unusual and tasty vegetable recipes in the world.

FOR THE BEST IN PAPERBACKS, LOOK FOR THE 🐧

THE PENGUIN COOKERY LIBRARY – A SELECTION

The Best of Eliza Acton   Selected and Edited by Elizabeth Ray
With an Introduction by Elizabeth David

First published in 1845, Eliza Acton's *Modern Cookery for Private Families*, of which this is a selection, is a true classic which everyone interested in cookery will treasure.

Easy to Entertain   Patricia Lousada

Easy to Entertain hands you the magic key to entertaining without days of panic or last minute butterflies. The magic lies in cooking each course ahead, so that you can enjoy yourself along with your guests.

French Provincial Cooking   Elizabeth David

'It is difficult to think of any home that can do without Elizabeth David's *French Provincial Cooking* . . . One could cook for a lifetime on the book alone' – *Observer*

The National Trust Book of Traditional Puddings   Sara Paston-Williams

'My favourite cookbook of the year. Engagingly written . . . this manages to be both scholarly and practical, elegant without pretension' – *Sunday Times*

The New Book of Middle Eastern Food   Claudia Roden

'This is one of those rare cookery books that is a work of cultural anthropology and Mrs Roden's standards of scholarship are so high as to ensure that it has permanent value' – Paul Levy in the *Observer*

FOR THE BEST IN PAPERBACKS, LOOK FOR THE 🐧

GARDENING IN PENGUINS

The Penguin Book of Basic Gardening   Alan Gemmell

From the perfect lawn to the flourishing vegetable patch: what to grow, when to grow and how to grow it. Given the garden, a beginner can begin on the day he buys this book with its all-the-year-round Gardener's Calendar.

The Pip Book   Keith Mossman

All you need is a pip and patience . . . 'The perfect present for the young enthusiast, *The Pip Book* should ensure that even the most reluctant avocado puts down roots and sends up shoots' – *The Times*

The Town Gardener's Companion   Felicity Bryan

The definitive book for gardeners restricted by the dimensions of their gardens but unrestrained by their enthusiasm. 'A fertile source of ideas for turning a cat-ridden concrete backyard into a jungle of soothing green' – *Sunday Times*

Water Gardening   Philip Swindells

A comprehensive guide to the pleasures and uses of expanses of water, however great or small in the garden. Includes advice on aquatic and marginal plants and the management of ornamental fish.

Beat Garden Pests and Diseases   Stefan Buczacki

An invaluable book, covering all types of plants, from seedlings to root vegetables . . . there is even a section on the special problems of green-houses.

The Englishman's Garden   Alvide Lees-Milne and Rosemary Verey

An entrancing guided tour through thirty-two of the most beautiful individual gardens in England. Each garden is lovingly described by its owner. Lavishly illustrated.

FOR THE BEST IN PAPERBACKS, LOOK FOR THE

GARDENING IN PENGUINS

The Adventurous Gardener   Christopher Lloyd

Prejudiced, delightful and always stimulating, Christopher Lloyd's book is essential reading for everyone who loves gardening. 'Get it and enjoy it' – *Financial Times*

The Magic Garden   Shirley Conran

The gardening book for the absolute beginner. 'Whether you have a window box, a patio, an acre or a cabbage patch . . . you will enjoy this' – *Daily Express*

The Cottage Garden   Anne Scott-James

'Her history is neatly and simply laid out; well-stocked with attractive illustrations' – *The Times*. 'The garden book I have most enjoyed reading in the last few years' – *Observer*

Growing Fruit   Mary Spiller

From blossom to harvest, through planting, pruning, picking and storing, in a small or large garden, plot or pot, here is an illustrated step-by-step guide to growing fruit of all kinds.

The Illustrated Garden Planter   Diana Saville

How to choose plants for your garden – to cover a wall, creep between paving, provide colour in summer – and to plan for collective effect or to overcome a difficult site. 650 plants are illustrated, in all over 900 described.

Organic Gardening   Lawrence D. Hills

The classic manual on growing fruit and vegetables without using artificial or harmful fertilizers. 'Enormous value . . . enthusiastic writing and off-beat tips' – *Daily Mail*